UNIVERSITIES AND COLLEGES IN THE UNITED ARAB EMIRATES

Books LLC®, Reference Series, Memphis, USA, 2011. ISBN: 9781155962917. www.booksllc.net. Copyright: http://creativecommons.org/licenses/by-sa/3.0/deed.en

Table of Contents

Military academies of the United Arab Emirates
The Military High School, Al-Ain 2

Nursing schools in the United Arab Emirates
Ras al-Khaimah Medical and Health Sciences University 2

Private universities and colleges in the United Arab Emirates
Al Ghurair University 3
American University in Dubai 5
University of Wollongong in Dubai ... 6

Public universities in the United Arab Emirates
United Arab Emirates University 7
Zayed University 8

Schools of medicine in the United Arab Emirates
Dubai Medical College for Girls 9
Gulf Medical University 9
UEIMS School of Medicine & Dentistry 9

Universities and colleges in Ajman
Ajman University of Science and Technology 10

Universities and colleges in Dubai
Birla Institute of Technology & Science, Pilani – Dubai 11
British University in Dubai 12
Canadian University of Dubai 13

Dubai International Academic City .. 13
Dubai Men's College 14
Dubai Pharmacy College 16
Dubai School of Government 16
ENGECON Dubai 17
Heriot-Watt University Dubai 17
Hogeschool-Universiteit Brussel 18
Institute of Islamic and Arabic Studies (Dubai) 18
Institute of Management Technology, Dubai 18
Institute of Management Technology, Ghaziabad 19
List of universities and colleges in Dubai 21
Mahatma Gandhi University 21
Rochester Institute of Technology, Dubai 23
Shaheed Zulfiqar Ali Bhutto Institute of Science and Technology 23
Tamkeen 24
The Emirates Academy of Hospitality Management 24
University of Dubai 25

Universities and colleges in Fujairah
Fujairah College 26

Universities and colleges in Ras al-Khaimah
George Mason University 26
Ittihad University 37
RAKCODS 37

Universities and colleges in Sharjah
American University of Sharjah 38

ECUoS 41
Etisalat University College 42
Skyline University College (Sharjah) 42
University City of Sharjah 43
University of Sharjah 43

Universities and colleges in the Emirate of Abu Dhabi
ALHOSN University 43
Abu Dhabi University 44
Al Ain University of Science and Technology 45
Masdar Institute of Science and Technology 45
Paris-Sorbonne University Abu Dhabi 46
Petroleum Institute 47
Shaikh Khalifa Bin Zayed Bangladesh Islamia School 47

Universities and colleges in the United Arab Emirates
Commission for Academic Accreditation 49
Hamdan Bin Mohammed e-University 49
Higher Colleges of Technology 49
List of universities and colleges in the United Arab Emirates 51
Ministry of Higher Education and Scientific Research of the United Arab Emirates 52
National Research Foundation 52

Introduction

Purchase of this book entitles you to a free trial membership in the publisher's book club at www.booksllc.net. (Time limited offer.) Simply enter the barcode number from the back cover onto the membership form. The book club entitles you to select from hundreds of thousands of books at no additional charge. You can also download a digital copy of this and related books to read on the go. Simply enter the title or subject onto the search form to find them.

Each chapter in this book ends with a URL to a hyperlinked online version. Type the URL exactly as it appears. If you change the URL's capitalization it won't work. Use the online version to access related pages, websites, footnotes, tables, color photos, updates. Click the version history tab to see the chapter's contributors. Click the edit link to suggest changes.

A large and diverse editor base collaboratively wrote the book, not a single author. After a long process of discussion and debate, the chapters gradually took on a neutral point of view reached through consensus. Additional editors expanded and contributed to chapters striving to achieve balance and comprehensive coverage. This reduced the regional or cultural bias found in many other books and provided access and breadth on subject matter otherwise little documented.

The Military High School, Al-Ain

The **Military High School**, located in Al Ain in the Emirate of Abu Dhabi, United Arab Emirates, is a military school operated by INTERED a subsidiary of the SABIS/ International School of Choueifat. It was opened in 2004 with the intention of educating local Emirati military cadets.

Source (edited): "http://en.wikipedia.org/wiki/The_Military_High_School,_Al-Ain"

Ras al-Khaimah Medical and Health Sciences University

Ras Al-khaimah Medical and Health Sciences University (RAKMHSU) is a new medical university in Ras al-Khaimah, United Arab Emirates. The university was established by the Ras Al Khaimah Human Development Foundation (RAK – HDF) under the leadership of His Highness Sheikh Saud bin Saqr al Qasimi, Crown Prince & Deputy Ruler of Ras Al Khaimah and Chancellor of the University. RAK-HDF is a joint venture of the Ras al-Khaimah Government, Al Ghurair Investments and ETA Ascon Group, Dubai.

Mission

RAK Medical and Health Sciences University is committed, through its offering of academic programs in the medical and health sciences fields, to prepare graduates who are able to develop critical skills in their practice and application of knowledge, equipping them with practical and clinical skills and knowledge and enabling them to make a valuable contribution to patient and health care as individuals and as responsible members of society. The University is also committed to contributing to the advancement of knowledge through its support for research conducted by its faculty and students, and the promotion of life long learning.

Colleges

- College of Medical Sciences.
- College of Dental Sciences.
- College of Pharmaceutical Sciences.
- College of Nursing.

College of Medical Sciences (MBBS)

College of Medical Sciences offers Bachelor of Medicine and Bachelor of Surgery (MBBS), comprising of 2 years of basic sciences, 3 years of clinical sciences and training and one year of internship.

The curriculum has been developed to provide learning opportunities enabling medical students to acquire fundamental knowledge, develop basic skills and appropriate principles relevant to health care in the context of the community.

The five year curriculum has been designed to follow system wise, integrated and problem based approach to medical science. It integrates basic sciences with clinical sciences to enable the students to apply their knowledge to health care and develop a professional and compassionate approach to the analysis and management of health care.

The MBBS program obtained Initial Accreditation from Ministry of Higher Education,UAE in July 2006 and the first academic session commenced in Oct 2006. Admission is in progress for the next academic session commencing Sept 2007.

College of Dental Sciences (BDS)

The Bachelor of Dental Surgery (B D S) program is of five years duration followed by one year of internship.

The program comprises six months of general education, two years of basic medical and dental sciences and two-and-half years of clinical dental sciences. This is followed by a year of dental internship.

The curriculum has been developed to provide learning opportunities enabling dental students to acquire fundamental knowledge, develop basic skills and appropriate principles relevant to oral health care in the context of the community.

The graduates of this program shall have opportunities to work in general practice, the community dental service, hospital practice, university teaching and research in various individual organizations.

The BDS program has obtained Initial Accreditation from Ministry of Higher Education & Scientific Research, UAE and admission is in progress for the academic session commencing September 2009.

College of Pharamacuetical Sciences (B Pharm)

Bachelor of Pharmacy (B Pharm), comprises 6 months of general education, one year of basic sciences, two-and-half years of pharmaceutical sciences and training and 6 months of Practice School. The total program duration is four and half years.

The curriculum has been developed to provide learning opportunities enabling pharmacy students to acquire fundamental knowledge, develop basic skills and appropriate principles relevant to health care in the context of the community. appropriate principles relevant to health care in the context of the community. pharmaceutical education, and to prepare for evidence based pharmacy practice in the changing health care environment of the 21st century by integrating basic sciences with pharma sciences to enable the students to apply their knowledge to health care.

B.Pharm program has obtained Initial Accreditation from Ministry of Higher Education and Scientific Research and admissions is in progress for the academic session commencing September 2007.

College of Nursing (B.Sc Nursing)

College of Nursing offers Bachelor of Science in Nursing (B.Sc Nursing) of four year duration.

The four year curriculum has been designed to provide quality education in nursing which is comparable to the international levels. It also ensures that each student is exposed to professional knowledge and practice through evidence–based learning and problem-solving approaches.

The B.Sc.Nursing program has obtained Initial Accreditation from Ministry of Higher Education & Scientific Research, UAE and admission is in progress for the academic session commencing September 2007.

Senior staff

- Dr S. Gurumadhva Rao (Vice Chancellor)
- Mr M. Riazuddin (Director - Finance & Administration)
- Dr Yasser Easa Hamad Al Nuaimi (Director - Clinical Education)
- Dr Syed Ahmed (Director - Global Relations)
- Dr Patricia Berwick (Director - Institutional Effectiveness)
- Dr Vijaya Kumardhas (Dean, College of Nursing)
- Dr B.G. Nagavi (Dean, College of Pharmacy)
- Dr S.R. Prabhu (Dean, College of Dental Sciences)

Student council

RAK MHS University encourages students to voice out their needs through Student Council. The Student Council shall represent the student body. The Student Council ensures a speedy acclimatization of new students to RAK MHS University by promoting healthy friendships. Student Council holds regular meetings to organize activities such as orientation, sports, cultural programs, competitions, and magazine publication.

Extracurricular activities

RAK MHS University organizes many social, cultural and entertainment programs. Students are encouraged to develop their interests and abilities, and to practice their hobbies through a variety of programs and activities. The University places a lot of emphasis on its extra curricular activities, and enables students to make good use of their leisure time through forming student cultural and scientific societies.

Sports

The sports facility at RAK MHSU meets the athletic needs of the students. The indoor facilities include volleyball, table tennis, fitness centre, and tennis. The football, basketball and tennis courts are located within the campus. The office of the Student Affairs organizes, and co-ordinates all the athletic events and sports activities.

Source (edited): "http://en.wikipedia.org/wiki/Ras_al-Khaimah_Medical_and_Health_Sciences_University"

Al Ghurair University

Al Ghurair University (AGU) is a private university located in Dubai, United Arab Emirates and founded by Al Ghurair. The university offers bachelor's degrees in Business Administration, Computer Information Systems, Computer Science and Engineering, Electrical and Electronics Engineering, and Interior Design.

The university was founded in 1999 for the purpose of serving the national and regional community through equipping the young generations with the necessary knowledge and skills to fit to the development and productivity of their communities. Al Ghurair University is licensed by the UAE Ministry of Higher Education and Scientific Research. All bachelor degree programs offered by AGU have been granted accreditation. Since its inception in 1999, AGU has always kept its sense of obligation to the community. AGU is a young and fast growing university, which is responsive to the dynamic changes of the local and regional markets. The university's educational programs foster students' learning that contributes to the development of the individual and society. In the past few years AGU attracted people from various nationalities and backgrounds, and the student base has expanded substantially in a well-set unity that encourages everyone to work together to achieve the ambitious goals and objectives of this institution.

Colleges and Departments

College of business studies

The College of Business Studies (COBS) provides high quality undergraduate education in the field of business administration. The College stimulates intellectual interest and business insight among its students by means of providing quality instruction, advising, and related support services. The College of Business Studies offers an intellectually challenging learning environment to enable students to build critical thinking, analytical ability, and communication skills to successfully assume managerial and leadership roles in today's knowledge-based global economy. The College is committed to maintaining international academic standards, multidisciplinary approaches, and using state-of-the art teaching methods, and technologies to broaden students' knowledge and equip them with appropriate skills, attitudes, and confidence to deal with real-world business problems. The College of Business Studies received initial accreditation from the CAA, Ministry of Higher Education and Scientific Research, U.A.E. in April 2004.

College of computing

At present **College of Computing** offers a B.S Computer Information Systems (CIS). The CIS curriculum is designed in such a way that majority of the courses have a practical lab component. In fact the graduates will have a strong ability to apply information technology to start a successful focused career with this knowledge and tools. Thus, they can carry on with their postgraduate studies or enter the market with confidence.

Objectives & goals

- Sound understanding of fundamentals – Students will have sound understanding of the foundation and specialization courses of their disciplines. Thus, they will be proficient in use of this knowledge to formulate and analyze problems, and synthesize and develop appropriate solutions.
- Tools for creativity – Graduates will possess the skills required in the design process, including the abilities to think, to communicate ideas effectively, to synthesize information and to formulate and solve problems.
- Preparation for Practice – Graduates will be prepared for practice in their disciplines and for graduate studies; they will be motivated to continue their education through lifelong professional development and learning.
- Societal Awareness – Graduates will be sensitive to the needs of society and will possess the ability to integrate practice of their disciplines into the social, economic, and entrepreneurial fields.
- Leadership Skills – Graduates will understand human nature and human institutions; they will be able to plan and manage projects, to work collaboratively, to communicate effectively with diverse groups, and interact with others on a professional/ethical basis.

Degrees offered

Bachelor of Science in Computer Information Systems (BS – CIS)

The program objectives are twofold, the first part deals with General Education Component, and the second part deals with the foundation and specialization courses. Through the foundation and specialization courses, the student will:

- Have the ability to apply information technology to business, services, and products.
- Have the capability to deploy and manage information technology resources and services in organizational process.
- Have knowledge and skills required to identify, formulate and solve problems throughout their career; *Have personal integrity, ethical behavior and cultural awareness in the practice of their profession; Be able to work closely with other professionals associate with computing.

College of engineering & applied sciences

The College provides students with an explicit description of the curricula and the academic goals and educational objectives of each of the engineering programs. As expected, these goals and objectives dictate the curricula and degree requirements. The undergraduate studies include a significant set of core courses that aim to endow the engineering graduates with competencies that transform them into thinking citizens and lifelong learners. Additionally, the aim is to enable all our students to assume positions of technical leadership and professional responsibility, and to achieve full satisfaction in their jobs, or in graduate studies, upon graduation from Al Ghurair University. Furthermore, we train our graduates to become energetic participants in the social changes brought about by engineering and technology, in the course of time.

Programs offered

A Bachelors of Science in Electrical and Electronics Engineering and a Bachelors of Science in Computer Science and Engineering

School of design

The School of Design provides students with the academic preparation for professional practice in both commercial and residential interior design. The Interior Design program has been recognized and accredited by Minster of Higher Education and recognized as being among "the best Interior Design schools in UAE". The Interior Design Program at Al Ghurair University embraces both residential and commercial design fields; the curriculum provides comprehensive coverage of all major areas of training including concept development, design, communication, presentation, construction and professional services and procedures. The Interior Design Bachelor of Arts degree program provides students with the technical, creative and critical thinking skills to enter the Interior Design profession. Courses encompass the study of design theory, aesthetics, history, graphics, lighting, space planning, interior construction and professional practice internships. Field trips, guest speakers and community service projects maintain strong connections to the profession and the region.

Recent Achievements

The University has added to its well equipped library & learning resources through subscription to a number of electronic databases - like ABI Inform, IEEE and ebrary. This makes latest publications and journals in the fields of business and engineering available to faculty and students. The university has also subscribed to Blackboard, a sophisticated Learning Management System, facilitating the use of advanced computer technology in teaching and learning.

Al Ghurair

Al Ghurair is a diversified industrial group based in Dubai with core focus on Foods, Commodities, Construction and Properties and additional sector focus within Energy, Printing, Retail and Education. With a market reach spanning more than 50 countries globally, Al Ghurair has a rich history of pioneering businesses and a heritage of success that is built upon values of excellence in the products developed and the processes followed.
- Al Ghurair

Source (edited): "http://en.wikipedia.org/wiki/Al_Ghurair_University"

American University in Dubai

The American University in Dubai (AUD) (Arabic: الجامعة الأمريكية في دبي) is a private, non-sectarian institution of higher learning in Dubai, United Arab Emirates, founded in 1995. AUD was founded in 1995 as a branch campus of the American InterContinental University in Atlanta, Georgia, but turned into a private, non-sectarian institution in 2007. AUD is accredited regionally as a separate unit by the Southern Association of Colleges and Schools. AUD serves UAE nationals and international students from all over the world and offer them world-class career-oriented education.

The University has both US and UAE accreditation for all of its programs. AUD prides itself for being the first University outside the United States and Latin America to be directly accredited by the Southern Association of Colleges and Schools. American University in Dubai is not affiliated with American University in Washington, D.C.

Academics

The University is organized into Schools and Departments:
- **School of Business Administration**
- **School of Engineering**
- **Mohammed bin Rashid School of Communication**
- **Department of Computer and Information Technology**
- **Department of Architecture**
- **Department of Visual Communication**
- **Department of Interior Design**
- **Division of Arts and Sciences**
- **Center for English Proficiency**

The campus

The American University in Dubai is situated next to Dubai Media City, Dubai Internet City, and the Palm Islands. It is 15 minutes from the heart of Dubai's financial and commercial centre and 25 minutes from Dubai International Airport.

AUD's multi-complex facility is situated on grounds of approximately 1,300,000 sq ft (121,000 m). and encompasses three academic buildings, a Student Center, an administration building, residence halls, a cafeteria area, and an open air sports facilities.

International accreditation

In December 2007, AUD received accreditation as a separate unit (independent of the American InterContinental University) by the Commission on Colleges of the Southern Association of Colleges and Schools (SACS) to award Bachelor's and Master's degrees. AUD is the only institution outside of the US and Latin America to be granted this honor by SACS.

Previously, from its founding in 1995, and until December 2007, AUD was only accredited by SACS as a branch campus of American InterContinental University (AIU). SACS later granted AUD separate unit accreditation. The Ministry of Higher Education and Scientific Research (Commission for Academic Accreditation) of the United Arab Emirates has also accredited various programs.

Visitors

- In 2009, Mahmoud Ahmadinejad visited AUD, and delivered a speech to the community.
- In 2009, Colin Powell delivered the commencement speech at the graduation ceremony.
- In 2008, Margaret Spellings delivered the commencement speech at the graduation ceremony.
- In 2007, Seymour Hersh delivered the commencement speech at the graduation ceremony.
- In 2006, Cherie Blair delivered the commencement speech at the graduation ceremony.
- In 2005, Bill Clinton delivered a speech and met with the Clinton Scholars at the university.
- In 2005, Christiane Amanpour delivered the commencement speech at the graduation ceremony.
- In 2004, Madeleine Albright delivered the commencement speech at the graduation ceremony.
- In 2003, Sandy Berger delivered the commencement speech at the graduation ceremony.
- In 2002, Bill Clinton delivered the commencement speech at the graduation ceremony.
- In 2001, George J. Mitchell delivered the commencement speech at the graduation ceremony.
- In 2000, Steve Forbes delivered the commencement speech at the graduation ceremony.
- In 1999, Ray LaHood delivered the commencement speech at the graduation ceremony.
- In 1998, James Baker delivered the commencement speech at AUD's first graduation ceremony.

Source (edited): "http://en.wikipedia.

org/wiki/American_University_in _Dubai"

University of Wollongong in Dubai

The University of Wollongong in Dubai (in Arabic: جامعة ولونغونغ في دبي) also known as **UOWD** is a private university located in Dubai, United Arab Emirates. University of Wollongong in Dubai (UOWD) is one of the UAE's oldest and most prestigious universities. As of 2009, the university had a total of 3,565 students from 99 countries.

Established in 1993 by University of Wollongong in Australia. UOWD represented a very early Australian initiative in the Gulf region. From a small beginning opposite Al Mulla Plaza, through its landmark presence on Jumeirah Road to its current location at Dubai Knowledge Village, the prestigious university is now recognized as being an integral part of Dubai.

As an independent UAE institution of higher education, UOWD attracts students not just from the UAE and Australia but from all over the world. Approximately 3,500 students representing almost a hundred nationalities are currently enrolled at UOWD and enjoy a quality academic experience.

UOWD offers a variety of specialist Undergraduate and Postgraduate programs in its three faculties – Business & Management, Finance & Accounting, and Computer Science & Engineering, which are directly linked to the human resource needs of the UAE.

All UOWD degree programs are accredited by the UAE Ministry of Higher Education and Scientific Research. In addition, the Australian Universities Quality Agency (AUQA) includes UOWD in its audits of UOW. The internationally recognised qualifications enable UOWD graduates to pursue rewarding careers in Dubai's burgeoning employment market. UOWD Alumni include many high profile graduates placed in prominent positions in both the public and private sectors across the region.

UOWD's Centre for Language & Culture offers language courses in English and Arabic. They range from English language study for University preparation to part time Arabic classes and English language teacher training. The Arabic program focuses on the linguistic as well as the cultural experience, enabling participants to explore and enjoy Dubai's diversity.

The University's faculty is a mix of locally and internationally recruited academics with extensive teaching, business and industry experience. They bring years of knowledge gained from research in their respective fields into the classroom providing students with a stimulating academic environment. Classes are small in number, allowing the lecturers to cater to the students' individual needs.

Since its inception, the University of Wollongong in Dubai has built a reputation for quality, credibility and integrity, and is held in high esteem by its students, alumni, business, industry and government. It maintains a long and proud tradition of excellence in education combined with liberal values of enquiry. It continuously strives to provide a fertile environment for bright young minds to flourish, where critical thinking is both encouraged and nurtured. These are the qualities that characterise great institutes of learning.

Campus

The University campus is located in Dubai, one of the seven emirates of the United Arab Emirates (UAE) and the Largest city in United Arab Emirates. It is situated at Dubai Knowledge Village, an educational free trade zones campus in the city of Dubai that provides facilities for training and learning institutions. In addition to the administrative building, the library, the university campus includes the faculties, student lounge and the Food Court which houses many different restaurants.

UOWD offer Residential Services to students, allowing them to live together in a unique multi-cultural environment conducive to academic success, personal growth, and social development. The Residences are located in Jebel Ali Gardens (approximately 15 minutes by bus from Dubai Knowledge Village) available only for females and Ewan Complex (approximately 40 minutes by bus from Dubai Knowledge Village).

Programs offered by UOWD

UOWD Front

Undergraduate

  * Bachelor of Business Administration
  * Bachelor of Commerce: Accountancy
  * Bachelor of Commerce: Finance
  * Bachelor of Commerce: Human Resource Management
  * Bachelor of Commerce: Management
  * Bachelor of Commerce: Marketing
  * Bachelor of Commerce: International Business
  * Bachelor of Computer Science
  * Bachelor of Computer Science in Multimedia Technology
  * Bachelor of Computer Science in Digital Systems Security (DSS)
  * Bachelor of Information Technology in Management Information Systems (MIS)
  * Bachelor of Internet Science and Technology
  * Bachelor of Engineering (Electrical, Computer Science, Telecommunications)*
  * Study Abroad @ UOWD

Postgraduate

* Master of Business Administration (MBA)
* Master of International Business (MIB)
* Master of Quality Management (MQM)
* Master of Strategic Marketing (MSM)
* Master of Strategic Human Resource Management (MSHRM)
* Master of Applied Finance and Banking (MAFB)
* Master of Engineering Management (MEM)
* Master of Information Technology Management (MITM)
* Master of Science (Logistics) MSc (Log)
* Doctor of Business Administration
* Doctor of Philosophy

Short Courses

* Certificates of Proficiency
    o Accounting for Managers
    o Marketing Management
    o International Business Strategy
    o Quality Management
    o Engineering Project Management
    o Information Technology Strategic Planning
    o Human Resource Management
    o Professional Certificate in Banking Risk Management
* Professional Certificates
    o Graduate Certificate in Forensic Accounting
    o Professional Certificate in Banking Risk Management
    o Certificate in Islamic Commercial and Investment Banking
    o Certificate in Fundamentals of Islamic Banking and Finance
    o Certificate in Business

Accreditation

All UOWD undergraduate and postgraduate degrees are accredited by the UAE Ministry of Higher Education and Scientific Research (Commission for Academic Accreditation). They are also audited by the Australian Universities Quality Agency.

Source (edited): "http://en.wikipedia.org/wiki/University_of_Wollongong_in_Dubai"

United Arab Emirates University

United Arab Emirates University (in Arabic: جامعة الإمارات العربية المتحدة) was established in 1976, and is the oldest of the three government-sponsored institutions of higher learning in the United Arab Emirates compared to the Higher Colleges of Technology and Zayed University. The university is located in Al Ain, United Arab Emirates. The university - in theory - upholds a strict criteria for admission to UAE nationals only, unlike other multiethnic universities in the country. In practice however, student crowds are mixed with a focus on Gulf and other Arab nationals.

Location

The university is located in the city of Al Ain, an oasis city in the Abu Dhabi emirate approximately 140 km east of the capital city.

Mission statement

United Arab Emirates University is the premier national university whose mission is to meet the educational and cultural needs of the UAE society by providing programs and services of the highest quality. It contributes to the expansion of knowledge by conducting quality research and by developing and applying modern information technology. It plays a significant role in leading cultural, social and economic development in the country.

Rankings

The United Arab Emirates University was ranked the 372nd best university in the world in the 2010 QS World University Rankings, with its life sciences programs ranked the 202nd best globally. In its capacity as a business school, UAEU was placed as the third best business school in Africa and the Middle East in the 2010 QS Global 200 Business Schools Report. In 2010, according to University Ranking by Academic Performance (URAP), it is the best university in the country and 894th university in the world.

Controversy

After several years of positive academic development such as increasing international accreditation for several faculties, the recruitment of research oriented faculty, and an expansion of postgraduate degree-offerings, the planned research orientation announced by the new Provost Dr. Rory Hume seems to have run out of steam. In an article in The Chronicle titled "Money Proves Elusive and Progress Difficult at United Arab Emirates U.", much information on the impending re-orientation can be found, with some comments below the article by the Provost and Emirati faculty.

The direction for the future of UAEU is somewhat unclear, though expectations seem mostly negative (The Chronicle forum or DAVE's ESL). Finally there is UAEUNIVERSITYWATCH, a recent watch site created by a collective of teaching staff concerned about the lack of clear strategic goals, erratic management, questionable academic standards as well as lack of intellectual freedom and human rights within UAE University.

Academics

The university comprises the following colleges:
* Faculty of Humanities and Social Sciences
* Faculty of Science
* Faculty of Education
* Faculty of Business and Economics
* Faculty of Law
* Faculty of Food and Agriculture
* Faculty of Engineering
* Faculty of Medicine and Health Science
* Faculty of Information Technology
* University General Requirements

Unit

Research

United Arab Emirates University is also engaged in numerous research and development projects. In 2003, the University has signed a scientific cooperation with University of California at Davis to enhance its role to drive the research and development sector in the United Arab Emirates.
Source (edited): "http://en.wikipedia.org/wiki/United_Arab_Emirates_University"

Zayed University

Zayed University (ZU), established in 1998, is the newest of the three government sponsored higher educational institutions in the United Arab Emirates. The other two institutions are the Higher Colleges of Technology established in 1988 and the United Arab Emirates University established in 1976. Zayed University was named in honor of Sheikh Zayed bin Sultan Al Nahyan, the country's first president and founder.

Academics

Zayed University is organized academically into six colleges: Arts and Sciences, Business Sciences, Communication and Media Sciences, Education, Information Technology and University College.

English is the medium of instruction except in courses in Arabic and Islamic studies. Because of this, students may need to spend up to two years in an English language preparatory program before entering the bachelor's program. The first two years in the university are in a general education program in University College (Colloquy), providing a broad grounding in the arts, humanities, and social sciences. Students then move into the majors which are housed in the colleges.

Research and outreach are given particular emphasis at ZU. A Research Incentive Fund provides up to US$325,000 in assistance annually to support research and scholarly and creative endeavors, stimulating ideas and interests which benefit faculty, the university and the UAE. ZU is increasingly hosting prestigious international events. In 2006, the Women as Global Leaders Conference, organized by Zayed University, attracted delegates from 88 countries and leading women speakers including Queen Rania of Jordan and former president of Ireland, Mary Robinson.

The university offers a number of graduate programs in administration, arts, business, communications, health care and education leadership, and science.

Outcomes-Based Academic Program Model

Zayed University had adopted an outcomes-based academic program model. The Colloquy and undergraduate programs at Zayed University are outcome-based and designed on the Zayed University Learning Outcomes. These six outcomes were created by faculty members at Zayed University as a means of developing the necessary skills to prepare students for continuous lifelong learning and future success in the world.

The Zayed University Learning Outcomes, as found in the Zayed University Catalog are:
1) Language: ZU graduates will be able to communicate effectively in English and Modern Standard Arabic, using the academic and professional conventions of these languages appropriately.
2) Information Technology: ZU graduates will be able to use current information technology to enhance productivity and effectiveness.
3) Critical Thinking and Quantitative Reasoning: ZU graduates will be able to use both critical and quantitative processes to solve problems and to develop informed opinions.
4) Information Literacy: ZU graduates will be able to find, evaluate and use appropriate information from multiple sources to respond to a variety of needs.
5) Global Awareness: ZU graduates will be able to understand and value their own and other cultures, perceiving and reacting to differences from an informed and socially responsible point of view.
6) Leadership: ZU graduates will be able to undertake leadership roles and responsibilities, interacting effectively with others to accomplish shared goals. (p. 9-10)

Once students enter their major program, their courses in the program are outcome-based designed on that major's Learning Outcomes, which prepare students for their future in that field. These major programs are housed within one of the six academic colleges; each college's faculty members have created its major Learning Outcomes aligned with the Zayed University Learning Outcomes.

Accreditation

On June 30, 2008, it was announced that Zayed University had been granted accreditation by the U.S.-based Commission on Higher Education of the Middle States Association of Colleges and Schools. In 2006, the College of Communication and Media Sciences had its Public Relations and Advertising major accredited by the International Advertising Association. This program has the distinction of being the only major program at Zayed University which has achieved full accreditation by an external agency.

Student Population

Zayed University has two campuses in the emirates of Abu Dhabi and Dubai, which collectively serve approximately 5,800 male and female students who take classes separately.

Campuses

The Dubai Campus moved to a new purpose-built location in September 2006. The new Abu Dhabi campus will be moving to a new campus in Khalifa City and is scheduled to open on July 31, 2011 in time for the fall 2011 semester. This new site was built at a cost of AED 3 billion and will have 3 main campus areas, 28 buildings, a sports complex, a residential building and a convention center all of which cover a total area of 18.8 hectares.

Controversies

In February 2006, Zayed University was at the heart of a major international controversy when one of its faculty members — Claudia Kiburz — distributed photocopies of a portrayal of the Prophet to encourage classroom discussion. This caused outrage among Muslims, and she was swiftly fired — a summary dismissal from Sheikh Nahyan, without any right to appeal.

In August 2008, Zayed University came under fire for allegedly implementing a divisive pay policy. According to the Abu Dhabi-based newspaper *The National*, local Emirati staff are to receive a 28% pay award, whereas foreign faculty will only receive 5%.

A salary freeze was imposed at ZU in May 2010. In January 2011, the National reported that Zayed University staff would be getting a 2 percent pay raise retroactive to August 2010, which reportedly would be their first pay raise in three and a half years

Awards

Zayed University was named one of the Top Ten Great Places/Companies to Work in for 2011.
Source (edited): "http://en.wikipedia.org/wiki/Zayed_University"

Dubai Medical College for Girls

Dubai Medical College for Girls is the first private college awarding degree of Medicine & Surgery in the United Arab Emirates, due to the foresight of Haj Saeed Lootah. This college was established in Dubai on an Islamic foundation to offer women in the UAE an opportunity to study medicine within the UAE.

History

The first students were admitted in 1985, and the Ministry of Higher Education and Scientific Research UAE recognised the college in 1994, and gave its degrees the equivalence of the MBBS in 1996. In 1995, the British Medical Council recognised the degrees awarded by the college.
Source (edited): "http://en.wikipedia.org/wiki/Dubai_Medical_College_for_Girls"

Gulf Medical University

Gulf Medical University (formerly **Gulf Medical College**) is based in Ajman. The college offers M.B.B.S., Bachelor of Physiotherapy, Pharm D and DMD undergraduate programs in addition to postgraduate and residency programs. Gulf Medical University is the first medical school in the region to offer admission to both males and females of all nationalities. Thumbay Moideen is the founder and president of this university established in 1998.

The college publishes the quarterly health magazine *GMC Health Journal*.

The Student General Council elections take place annually for which one general secretary and two joint secretaries are appointed. The Student Council has had a strong bearing on college events and activities. The college hails the elected general secretaries by displaying their names at the main hall university entrance.

Work is currently underway for the construction of a gym (Body & Soul), swimming pool, auditorium, staff accommodation and another hospital in the main university campus.

Gulf Medical College Ajman is promoted by Thumbay Group U.A.E.
Source (edited): "http://en.wikipedia.org/wiki/Gulf_Medical_University"

UEIMS School of Medicine & Dentistry

UEIMS was a university banned by the government of UAE for illegal practices and fraudulent services. The institutions under Sudhir Gopi Holdings were:
- UEIMS School of Medicine & Dentistry, Ras Al Khaimah, UAE
- Mahatma Gandhi University Off Campus Center, Dubai International Academic City, Dubai, UAE
- Indira Gandhi National Open University Center, Dubai International Academic City, Dubai, UAE

UEIMS School of Medicine & Dentistry had claimed to provide education in the fields of medicine and dentistry based on combination of humanized needs blended with undistorted international standards and the most advanced medical practices which are effective and best suited to contemporary health care practice. The mission of UEIMS School of Medicine & Dentistry was said to have been to create global citizens equipped to be successful in demanding global careers. UEIMS used to have nearly 300 students on its rolls. The geographic distribution of the students wer mostly from (India, Pakistan, South Africa, Kenya, Nigeria, Egypt, Iran, Iraq, Kuwait, Qatar, Bahrain, Saudi Arabia and Oman.). Students were said to have been enrolled into the program without any regard to gender, national/ethnic origin or religion.

Sudhir Gopi Holdings Inc, had claimed to provide MBBS, MD, BDS, Engineering, Management, IT and Fashion Technology programs for students from all over the world. The students enrolled in institutions under SG Holdings, in India, Dubai, Ras Al Khaimah UAE and Philippines. Sudhir Gopi Holdings had established facilities in Dubai prior to govenment investigation.

MBBS program

UEIMS School of Medicine & Dentistry was said to have been affiliated to the International University of the Health Sciences (IUHS) located at St Kitts, West Indies (Caribbean Islands), until its investigation by the government of UAE. Registration, Examination, Evaluation and Certification of MBBS program was said to have been done by IUHS. IUHS is listed in the WHO (World Directory of Medical Schools).

The program was supposed be of 4½ years duration (2 years of Pre-clinical Training & 2 ½ years of Clinical Training), atypical of most accredited medical schools. On successful completion of the 4½ years program, the student expected to be certified as Bachelor of Medicine and Bachelor of Surgery (MBBS) by IUHS, St Kitts which is recognized by the Government of St Christopher and Nevis and is also listed in the WHO World Directory of Medical Schools.

The fraudulent practices have resulted in a large public outcry.

BDS program

The program was claimed to have been of 4½ years duration (2 years of Pre-clinical Training & 2 ½ years of Clinical Training). On successful completion of the 4 ½ years program, students had expected to be certified as Bachelor of Dental Surgery (BDS).

Eligibility

The Candidates all had to be at least 17 years of age as on the date of admission.

Key personnel at UEIMS School of Medicine & Dentistry

- Sudhir Gopi (Chairman & Managing Director). Mr Sudhir Gopi was once a certified Attorney with a graduate degree in Law and a post-graduate degree in Business Administration. Before he ventured into his medical certificate business, Mr Gopi had practiced law at various Indian courts. He founded Sudhir Gopi Holdings in the year 1998. Sudhir Gopi Holdings still exists as of February 2011, despite closures of its Dubai offices.
- Praveen Kumar A. R (Director - Operations). While UEIMS still existed, Mr Praveenkumar functioned as the Operations Director of Sudhir Gopi Holdings. He has a Bachelor's Degree in Commerce with a Post-Graduate Degree in Business Administration. Mr Praveenkumar has been associated with the Group right from its initial days.
- Vinu Tarur (Director). Mr Vinu is a Graduate in Commerce from Calicut University (Kerala) with a postgraduate degree in Management. Mr Vinu is in charge of the activities at the Rajagiri International School and UEIMS School of Medicine & Dentistry. Before joining the Group 3 years ago, Mr Vinu was associated with a pharmacy company for over 8 years.
- Ram Kumar Ram Mohan (Principal – Dentistry). Dr Ramkumar Rammohan was heading the Dental Department at UEIMS School of Medicine and Dentistry. A maxillofacial surgeon by profession, Dr Ramkumar obtained his Masters in Dental Surgery from the Meenakshi Ammal Dental College in Chennai. He has 14 years of clinical experience coupled with more than 9 years of teaching experience at both UG and PG levels.

Source (edited): "http://en.wikipedia.org/wiki/UEIMS_School_of_Medicine_%26_Dentistry"

Ajman University of Science and Technology

The **Ajman University of Science and Technology (AUST)** is a technology-oriented university in Ajman, United Arab Emirates. The university was founded in 1988 as a university college. Notable alumni include Yaser Birjas.

Vision

In today's world, the forces of globalization and new technology impose an increasingly uniform model of society, a model which in some respects threatens the cultural diversity and heritage of humanity. Now, more than ever before, nations need universities which have a comprehensive vision, a vision which reflects national ambitions for progress and modernity yet at the same time preserves national culture, traditions and identity.

As an institution which promotes a new and active role for education in society, Ajman University of Science and Technology Network (AUSTN) seeks to adopt positive aspects of modernity. AUSTN believes that teaching, research and training practice need to constantly evolve, and for that to happen an environment open to innovation is required – an environment which fosters creativity and favors the emergence of centers of excellence. Such an environment also requires an excellent infrastructure which actively promotes academic communication and interaction.
- Education

- Information
- Investment

Ajman University Colleges
- College of Engineering
- College of Information Technology
- College of University Requirements and Academic Counseling
- College of Dentistry
- College of Information, Mass Communication and Humanities
- College of Pharmacy and Health Sciences
- College of Business Administration
- Institute of Environment, Water & Energy
- College of Education & Basic Sciences
- College of Law

Ajman University Library and Learning Resource Center

The goals and objectives of AUST's library and LRCs are to:
- Provide current library materials and databases that support the academic curriculum
- Provide access to information resources, regardless of location
- Collect library materials in all formats, broaden and update all collections to meet the needs of AUST's programs and support #the various aspects of the institution: teaching, training, research and services
- Educate and assist faculty, students and staff in the identification and effective use of information resources
- Continue to strengthen and update all collections to meet the needs of AUST programs
- Preserve AUST's collections and materials, and maintain and upgrade physical and technological infrastructure to enhance the #quality of services
- Recognize that a minimum expectable standard is one resource per topic per student
- Meet or exceed accreditation standards
- Provide access to library resources and servers via web pages and online recourses
- Ensure that resources available are current appropriate and accessible 24/7
- Work closely with users; know their needs and interests
- Put into practice the motto that building library resources is a continuous process
- Enhance information literacy, especially in the student community, by developing effective plans aiming at improving student ability to:
  - Access information effectively and efficiently
  - Evaluate information and its sources critically
  - Understand economic, legal and social issues when using information
  - Access and use information critically and legally

Source (edited): "http://en.wikipedia.org/wiki/Ajman_University_of_Science_and_Technology"

Birla Institute of Technology & Science, Pilani – Dubai

Birla Institute of Technology & Science, Pilani–Dubai (Hindi: बिरला प्रौद्योगिकी एवं विज्ञान संस्थान, पिलानी-दुबई) (Known as: **BITS, Pilani-Dubai** and **BPDC**) is a private technical University located in Dubai, United Arab Emirates. It is a campus of the Birla Institute of Technology & Science.

BITS, Pilani - Dubai at Dubai International Academic City was inaugurated by the Indian Insustrialist Krishna Kumar Birla on 5 December 2007.

It should not be confused with the Birla Institute of Technology, Mesra, which is a completely different university.

Highlights

- Spread over 14 acres (57,000 m), the institute is located at Dubai International Academic City
- World class infrastructure with state-of-the-art laboratories for Science and Engineering, mechanical engineering block cum workshop, sports facilities etc.
- Spacious Academic Block with Central Library.
- Practice school offered at reputed companies in UAE.
- Six Hostels (5 boys' and 1 girls) with fully furnished single-seater rooms, and mess facility.
- Academic flexibility like Dual Degree offered.
- Scholarships under various categories based on merit and need.

Academics

BITS, Pilani-Dubai offers the same courses as BITS, Pilani.

Dual Degree

One of the most popular flexibilities provided in the BITS, Pilani's educational structure is the Dual Degree Scheme. Under this scheme, it is possible for a student to work for and complete two Degrees within a reasonable period of time. All the admitted students are given an opportunity to take up a Dual Degree based on their performance in the first year of the programme.

Programmes offered

BITS, Pilani - Dubai International Academic City, Dubai

BITS Pilani-Dubai offers 4-year Integrated First Degree programs at the undergraduate level in the 7 following fields:
- B.E (Hons.) Chemical Engineering
- B.E (Hons.) Electrical & Electronics Engineering
- B.E (Hons.) Electronics & Communication Engineering
- B.E (Hons.) Electronics and Instrumentation Engineering

- B.E (Hons.) Mechanical Engineering
- B.E (Hons.) Computer Science Engineering.
- B.E (Hons.) Biotechnology

Higher degree evening programs offered are:
- M.Sc.(Tech.) Engineering Technology
- M.Sc.(Tech.) Information Systems
- M.E. Design Engineering
- M.E. Microelectronics
- M.E. Software Systems
- M.E. Biotechnology
- M.B.A. Engineering and Technology Management
- M.B.A. IT Enabled Services Management

Admissions and Scholarships

Admission to BITS, Pilani - Dubai Campus(BPDC) is based entirely on the candidates merit, his/her preferences, facilities available and availability of seats in the discipline preferred. The merit position of the candidate for admission will be based only on the overall aggregate secured by the candidate in the Qualifying Examination and not based on any entrance test. While the Dubai Campus has been setup especially to cater to the educational requirements of the residents of the GCC (Gulf Cooperation Council) countries, candidates from other countries are also eligible to apply. Admissions are open to all nationalities.

Scholarships

Meritorious and students with excellent sports achievements are awarded financial aid for their study at BPD, on the following categories:
- Merit Scholarship for students securing above 90 % and 80 % in the qualifying examination.
- Scholarship for Higher Secondary Board Toppers from different states/boards.
- Scholarship for sports excellence.
- BITSAT Scholarship for candidated with outstanding performance in BITS Admission Test (BITSAT)
- Merit-cum-means Scholarship

Academic and Research Collaboration

BITS Pilani-Dubai Campus has entered into research collaboration with the International Center for Biosaline Agriculture, Dubai, UAE

BPDC has also established Academic Collaborations with reputed American and Canadian universities.

Former Academic Block, BITS, Pilani - Dubai

- Purdue University, West Lafayette, Indiana, U.S.A.
- University of Maryland, College Park, U.S.A.
- Kansas State University (KSU), Manhattan, Kansas, U.S.A.
- Iowa State University of Science and Technology, Ames, Iowa, U.S.A.
- University at Buffalo, The State University of New York, USA
- George Mason University, Fairfax, Virginia, USA
- University of Ontario, Canada
- University of Windsor, Canada

The scope of Academic colloboration includes;
- Preferential admission into graduate programmes for BITS Pilani Dubai Campus students
- joint research activities
- Credits transfer
- Student and faculty exchange

Directors of BITS Pilani Dubai Campus

BITS, Pilani-Dubai was headed for 10 years since its inception by Prof.M. Ramachandran. Prof.R. K. Mittal became the Director on 16 July 2010.

Facilities

The Institute is located in Dubai International Academic City and offers excellent infra-structure and state-of-the art academic facilities to its students. Sports facilities however are in an extremely dilapidated state. Apart from the various facilities offered to the students on the campus, the Institute also provides Student visas, Hostel facilities and Transport facilities.

Relocation

BITS, Pilani - Dubai , was first located in Al Ghurair University Campus, then at Dubai Knowledge Village, and to its permanent campus with student housing at Dubai International Academic City in September 2007.

Other campuses

- Pilani Campus
- Goa Campus
- Hyderabad Campus

Source (edited): "http://en.wikipedia.org/wiki/Birla_Institute_of_Technology_%26_Science,_Pilani_%E2%80%93_Dubai"

British University in Dubai

The **British University in Dubai** (BUiD), was established in 2004, located in Dubai International Academic City, Dubai. is the Middle East region's first, research based, postgraduate university. BUiD offers a unique opportunity for higher education.

Working in partnership with leading UK universities BUiD offers education and research in key disciplines. BUiD has partnerships with the University of Edinburgh, the University of Manchester, the University of Birmingham, Cardiff University and the Cass Business School of City University, London. All BUiD Masters programmes have accreditation eligibility from UAE Ministry of Higher Education and Scientific Research .

BUiD's Founders and Contributors
BUiD was established as a 'not for prof-

it' University. The Founders of the University are Al Maktoum Foundation, Dubai Development and Investment Authority, the National Bank of Dubai, the British Business Group, and Rolls Royce.

BUiD has also received strong backing from local and international organisations who have shown their support for BUiD at several levels including funding and scholarships. These include the Emirates Group, DUCAB, Dubai Duty Free, DUGAS, Atkins, Hyder Consulting, and the Emirates Foundation.

Offered Programmes
MSc Information Technology
MSc Information Technology Management
MSc Project Management
Master of Education - Special Education; English Language Teaching; International Management and Policy
MEd Intensive Programme
MSc Environmental Design of Buildings
MSc Finance and Banking
=
Source (edited): "http://en.wikipedia.org/wiki/British_University_in_Dubai"

Canadian University of Dubai

The **Canadian University of Dubai** is an institution of higher education in Dubai, United Arab Emirates. Established in 2006, the school offers undergraduate and graduate programs.

History
The Canadian University of Dubai was established in September 2006 with no more than 100 students in September 2006. As of autumn 2009, the university serves over 1700 students of 90 nationalities.

Campus
The university is located at the center of Dubai behind the Shangri-la Hotel on Sheikh Zayed Road.

Organization and administration
The university has partnerships with other colleges and universities in various countries. These include Centennial College, University of New Brunswick, Athabasca University, Georgian College, and Niagara College in Canada; University of Marne la Vallée, Institut Supérieur d'Électronique et du Numérique, École de management de Lyon, École supérieure de commerce de Troyes, and Lumière University Lyon 2 in France; and Dublin Business School and Griffith College in Ireland.

Academics
The Canadian University of Dubai is accredited by the Ministry of Higher Education and Scientific Research. The university offers thirteen accredited degree programs with an additional six programs under development. Four schools currently comprise the university: the School of Business, the School of Architectural Studies & Interior Design, the School of Engineering, Applied Science and Technology, and the School of Environment & Health.
Source (edited): "http://en.wikipedia.org/wiki/Canadian_University_of_Dubai"

Dubai International Academic City

Dubai International Academic City (DIAC), is the new development currently under construction near Al Ruwayyah along the Dubai-Al Ain Road in the city of Dubai, United Arab Emirates. DIAC is located within Dubai Academic City, which spreads over an area of 129,000,000 square feet (12,000,000 m), and the development is scheduled to be completed by 2012. The project was launched in May 2006 as an area where educational institutions from with Dubai Knowledge Village will move to. The purpose of DIAC is to be a base for schools, colleges and universities. Due to the economic climate, an AED700m student accommodation, scheduled to be complete in September 2011 to house 2,800 students, will now be completed in early 2012. However, in 2009, a food court and student activity center were built. More than 12,000 students study in 13 international higher education institutes in DIAC. By 2015, Dubai Academic City expects to have 40,000 students.

Institutions at DIAC
- Al Ghurair University
- American University in Dubai
- American University in the Emirates
- Azad University
- Birla Institute of Technology & Science, Pilani - Dubai
- British University in Dubai
- Dubai Aerospace University
- Dubai Aviation College
- Dubai English Speaking College
- French Fashion University Dubai
- French School Dubai, secondary school
- German School Dubai, primary school
- Hamdan eTQM University
- Heriot Watt University Dubai
- Higher Colleges of Technology, Dubai Men's College campus
- Hult International Business School Dubai
- Institute of Management Technology Dubai
- JSS Academy Dubai
- Mahatma Gandhi University Dubai
- Manipal University Dubai
- Michigan State University Dubai
- Murdoch University Dubai
- National Institute for Vocational Education Dubai
- Rochester Institute of Technology Dubai
- St Joseph University Dubai
- S P Jain Center of Management Dubai

- SZABIST Dubai
- UAE Academy of Hospitality
- Universal Empire Institute of Medical Sciences
- Universal Empire Institute of Technology
- University of Waterloo Dubai
- Zayed University Academic City

Institutions expected to establish in or move to DIAC
- Colleges and universities currently based at DKV (Dubai Knowledge Village)
- American University in Dubai (currently near Hard Rock Cafe)
- Dubai Aviation College (currently near Garhood Bridge)
- Dubai Police Officers' Academy, (currently between Burj Al Arab and Sheikh Zayed Road)
- Dubai University College
- Institute of Management Technology, Dubai
- International Centre for Biosaline Agriculture
- St Petersburg State University of Engineering and Economics
- UAE Academy of Hospitality

Source (edited): "http://en.wikipedia.org/wiki/Dubai_International_Academic_City"

Dubai Men's College

Dubai Men's College (DMC), one of the first Higher Colleges of Technology (HCT), is a government-funded higher education institution located in Academic City, Dubai, in the United Arab Emirates (UAE). HCT, the largest higher education institution in the UAE, was established in 1988 and was designed to educate and empower UAE nationals. DMC is committed to providing the highest quality, career-oriented education in a dynamic and positive atmosphere that encourages creativity, intellectual fluency and constructive thought.

DMC provides Bachelor and Associate degrees in the fields of applied communications, business and financial services, electrical and civil engineering technology, health sciences, and information technology. English is the medium of instruction. A foundation program has been designed to equip students with the knowledge and skills required to be successful in a challenging higher education environment. On completion of the foundation year students may select from more than 30 programs. These programs are geared to the needs of the public and private sector in both the region and the world at large. Industry advisory boards assist the College and the Higher Colleges system in setting relevant skill requirements, which in turn are benchmarked against international academic standards. From September 2009, HCT's executive MBA program will be offered at the DMC campus.

The annual average enrollment is 2000 students and as of mid 2009, 5,372 students have graduated from the college. Many of these graduates now hold senior positions both in UAE government institutions and private industry and are making a substantial contribution to the growth of the UAE and regional economy.

In the 2008/09 academic year the college enrolled 384 foundation students, 424 diploma students, 833 higher diploma students, 274 bachelor students and employed 111 faculty. In total DMC has 200 staff members from 20 different countries. This provides a cosmopolitan environment which enhances the global awareness of the students and helps prepare them for the realities of modern life.

Over the years DMC has gained a widespread reputation of excellence and quality in applied and professional education. The strong ties developed with business and industry entities ensure rewarding employment opportunities for graduates. 98% of the 2007/08 graduating class was employed in their chosen field according to a poll conducted in November 0f 2008. Many organizations and corporations have entered into partnerships with DMC to provide development and training programs for their particular workforce.

History

DMC was established in 1989 by His Excellency Nahayan Mabarak Al Nahayan, UAE Minister of Higher Education and Scientific Research and Chancellor of the HCT, as one of the first four Higher Colleges of Technology in the country. DMC's first home was a former car show room. With nine classrooms, two twenty-station computer labs, an electronics lab, a physics lab and a civil engineering lab, the college welcomed its first batch of 95 students on 9 September 1989. Programs were offered in the business and technology fields with a foundations program to assist those students who needed to improve their language and numerical skills before entering a specialized field. The college was located on the Dubai-Sharjah road, near Dubai Airport. This provided a good opportunity not only for Dubai students but also for students from the nearby emirates to attend the college.

The original college building soon proved to be too small to accommodate the needs of the growing number of students and in 1991 the foundations program moved to an annex of its own. By 1995 there were three campuses- the main campus for career programs, the foundations campus and the BM campus for first year business students.

In Aug 1995, the college moved to the Al Mamzar building where all three campuses were combined into one. As the college enrollment progressed at a rapid rate year by year, by 1995, the year in which the certificate diploma course was introduced, it was no longer possible to accommodate the whole student body in one building. Thus in 1996 the foundations program moved to an annex of its own, followed by the communications technology in 1997. A learning centre was then added to the college facilities. In 1998 the college moved its premises to the former Dubai Women's College building near the Abu Hail Centre and finally in 2004, DMC moved to a new purpose-built campus at its current location, and was the first college to open its gates in Academic City.

Organization

As one of the Higher Colleges, DMC is governed by the central administration of HCT headed by the Vice Chancellor, Dr Tayeb Kamali. The College Senior Director, Dr Robert Richards, is responsible for the educational leadership and management of the college and reports to the Vice Chancellor. The college management committee consisting of the senior director, associate director, academic chairs and staff representatives forms the college administrative team. DMC today has four academic divisions with 6 departments.

- Business, IT and Applied Communications
- Foundations and English
- Engineering, Civil Construction, Electronics
- Learning Innovation : Educational Technology, In-Service Teacher Education, Academic Quality Assurance, Pastoral Development.

The college support departments include, Career Development and Industrial Alliances, Corporate Training and Graduate Studies, Entrepreneurship and Applied Research, Community and Public Relations, Academic and Student Services, Information Technology Services, Human Resources and Finance and Administration.

Program relevance is maintained with the participation of the Employer Advisory Committees for each program in the college. They meet regularly to ensure that the needs of industry are incorporated into the various programs. The college has established links with tertiary educational institutions and validating bodies in other countries in order to maintain international program standards and to facilitate the transfer of DMC graduates to programs of advanced study abroad.

Sports

DMC has excellent sports facilities that help the students to maintain and improve their health and fitness. Intramural and intercollegiate competitions within departments of the college and among the colleges of HCT and other colleges and universities are a regular occurrence. DMC students participate in College Olympic events, HCT Sports Day, the Higher Education Sports Federation (HESF) intercollegiate competitions, HCT rowing competitions and HCT cross country running. DMC students are highly successful in national championships in track and field, taekwondo, swimming, football, basketball, volleyball and table tennis. During the 2007-08 academic year, DMC won the HESF championship securing for themselves seven gold medals, the HCT overall championship, the HCT soccer league, and the HCT volleyball league.

The DMC sports and fitness center opened in 2004, making a significant difference to the capacity and quality of DMC's sporting activities. The 100,000 square-meter facility features an Olympic-size swimming pool, an outdoor multipurpose stadium, a FIFA approved soccer pitch, two 5-a side soccer pitches, a volleyball court, four tennis courts, a running track and field, two basketball courts, three squash courts, a cricket pitch, two beach soccer pitches, two beach volleyball pitches, an adventure quest site, two fully equipped gyms and a games room for playing snooker, billiards and table tennis.

The DMC Learning Centre

The DMC Learning Centre houses more than 35,000 books and 200 journals, magazines and newspapers. Textbooks and reference books support the college courses but books of fiction, popular videos, DVDs and graded readers are available on loan. A wide range of on-line databases that contain thousands of articles from magazines, newspapers, journals and reference books are also accessible to both students and staff. The Learning Centre is divided into 8 'zones'. These zones provide students and staff with a wide range of subject-specific resources within the various program areas. In addition to each program zone there is a leisure zone, reference zone, English zone and mathematics zone. The leisure zone is an area where students can relax, play board games, read newspapers and general interest magazines, access general fiction or readers, Arabic books, DVDs and videos. The reference zone has a large selection of encyclopedias, atlases and dictionaries on various topics. The English and mathematics zones offer extensive, up-to-date resources and professional help for the English language and math needs of DMC students.

Student services and activities

The Student Services department carries out a variety of tasks from helping new students in the transition from school to college life to finding suitable jobs for them on graduation. The student services department provides career counseling and career guidance to help students choose appropriate programs and subsequently suitable jobs. Work experience opportunities for students are offered through the career development centre. A wide range of extracurricular activities are offered throughout the academic year. Student activities are generally organized by the Dubai Men's College Student Administration Council and sporting activities by the sports section. Some of the college events organized last year include the iftar party, the Ramadan sports festival, international day, World Challenge, National Day and the mathematics rally. Many student clubs such as the art club, photography club, environmental club, chess club, anime and gaming club, billiards and snooker club, bowling club, mathematics club, Japan club, martial arts club, toastmasters' club, squash club and formula one racing club are also organized during out-of-college hours.

Scholarship program

DMC has a scholarship program to assist students with financial difficulties. The program has been developed with the cooperation of other organizations in the community and supported by His Excellency Sheikh Nahayan Mabarak Al Nahayan, UAE Minister of Education and Research and Chancellor of the HCT. The Mohammed bin Rashid Al Maktoum Foundation has been a continuous provider of assistance to students at Dubai Men's College. A Board of Trustees awards scholarships on the basis of merit and need.

Some notable alumni

DMC has produced many highly successful alumni. Among the best-known are:
- Chief Project Officer at Dubai Culture and Arts Authority Saeed Mohamed Ali Al Nabouda,
- Deputy CEO at Shaikh Mohammed bin Rashid Establishment Abdulbasit Mohamed Abdulla Al Janahi,
- Director of Jebel Ali Customs Mattar Al Mari,
- General Manager – Operations at MAF Investments LLC Fouad S Mansoor,
- Sharaf Group Director of Business Development at Sultan Group Investments LLC Jamal Qassim Sultan Albanna,
- Project Manager at the Prime Minister's Office Azzan Lootah,
- Chief Executive Officer of Amlak Finance Arif Alharmi,
- Captain Boeing 777 and Pilot Cadet Recruitment Manager of Emirates Airlines Abdulla Al Hammadi,
- Minister Advisor at the Ministry of Justice, Abdulla Abduljabbar Mohamed Al Majed,
- Manager of DubaiSat-1 Programme Emirates Institution of Advanced Science and Technology Salim Al Marri,
- Executive Director of Dubai Internet City Malek Sultan Al Malek.

Source (edited): "http://en.wikipedia.org/wiki/Dubai_Men%27s_College"

Dubai Pharmacy College

The **Dubai Pharmacy College** is the first pharmacy institution in the United Arab Emirates, established in 1992 by Dubai philanthropist Haji Saeed Bin Ahmed Al Lootah. In 2005, it won the Dubai Quality Appreciation Programme award for education presented by Sheikh Mohammed bin Rashid Al Maktoum, Crown Prince of Dubai.

Source (edited): "http://en.wikipedia.org/wiki/Dubai_Pharmacy_College"

Dubai School of Government

The **Dubai School of Government** is a research and teaching institution in Dubai, United Arab Emirates, which focuses on public policy in the Arab world. The School was established in 2005 under the patronage of HH Sheikh Mohammed Bin Rashid Al Maktoum, Vice President and Prime Minister of the United Arab Emirates and Ruler of Dubai.

According to the School's Web site, it *"aims to promote good governance through enhancing the region's capacity for effective public policy."*

The School works to achieve its mission through a four-pronged approach, including applied research in public policy and management, academic programs in public policy and public administration, executive education programs, and knowledge forums for scholars and policy makers.

Applied Research

The School conducts applied research in public policy and management, focusing on areas such as organizational development, public sector management, gender and public policy, e-government, education, economics, labor and demographics and disability policy. Research is conducted with an eye to academic rigor and to policy relevance for the Arab world.

DSG has an active series of publications, consisting primarily of policy briefs, working papers and reports.

Academic programs

On December 16, 2009, the School graduated its first cohort of 32 students in an intensive, one-year Master of Public Administration program. Designed for mid-level public sector professionals, the MPA program is designed to train students in the modern theory and techniques of public sector management, and to help them better understand the political and social context in which public policies are designed and implemented and public services are provided. The MPA is conducted in coordination with the Harvard Kennedy School's Faculty Advisory Committee.

DSG also offers an Executive Diploma in Public Administration (EDPA) in partnership with the Lee Kuan Yew School of Public Policy at the National University of Singapore..

All DSG academic programs are officially accredited by the UAE Ministry of Higher Education and Scientific Research.

Executive Education

The School conducts both customized and open executive education programs through its faculty and in cooperation with the Kennedy School of Government at Harvard University and the Lee Kuan Yew School of Public Policy at the National University of Singapore. Executive education clients have included organizations within the Dubai Government, as well as governments throughout the Arab world.

In May 2008, the School signed a Memorandum of Understanding to provide academic and training programs for Egyptian government officials. A similar agreement was reached in July 2008 with the Government of Syria, and discussions are ongoing with officials in other governments throughout the Arab world.

Public Affairs

The School provides a platform for public dialogue and knowledge exchange by convening conferences, lectures, seminars and policy forums. DSG's Distinguished Speakers Series has featured guests such as Lee Kuan Yew, Klaus Schwab, Lawrence Summers, John Chambers, David Ellwood, Joseph Nye, Francis Fukuyama, Suad Joseph, Kishore Mahbubani and Bob Graham, to name a few.

Recent conferences have included "Best Practices in Entrepreneurship Policy" (November 2009), "Healthcare Challenges in the GCC" (November 2009) and "Natural Resources and Economic Development: Risks and Policy Challenges" (December 2009).

The School also hosts a Research Seminar Series, which brings together academics and researchers from different and often varying backgrounds, serving as a focal point for the identification and consolidation of research interests.

The Dubai Initiative

The Dubai School of Government works in close cooperation with the Kennedy School of Government at Harvard University. This joint partnership, known as the Dubai Initiative, includes funding, coordinating and facilitating fellowships, internships, faculty and graduate research grants, working papers, multi-year research initiatives, conferences, symposia, public lectures, policy workshops, faculty workshops, case studies and customized executive education programs.

The Middle East Youth Initiative

The Middle East Youth Initiative (MEYI) is a partner initiative that was launched by the Wolfensohn Center for Development at the Brookings Institution and the Dubai School of Government in July 2006. According to the Initiative's Web site, "*the mission of the Initiative is to develop and implement a regional action plan for promoting the economic and social inclusion of young people in the Middle East.*"

In November 2009, the Initiative released *Generation in Waiting: The Unfulfilled Promise of Young People in the Middle East*. Edited by Tarik Yousef and Navtej Dhillon, the book represents three years of research on youth exclusion in the Middle East. Bringing together perspectives from the Maghreb to the Levant, the volume is an essential resource for researchers, policymakers, civil society and private sector leaders hoping to better understand the opportunities and challenges facing the region's youth demographic.

In 2009, MEYI embarked on a new partnership with Silatech to generate solutions in critical youth areas by promoting new knowledge, innovation, and learning across borders. Silatech is a Qatar-based initiative that aims to improve the social and economic status of young people through the creation of progressive, entrepreneurial markets, and employment and business opportunities globally and in the Arab world.

More info. about DSG

Who's Who at the Dubai School of Government
    DSG's Public Affairs Programs
    DSG in the News
    Watch & Listen to DSG lectures and Public forums
Source (edited): "http://en.wikipedia.org/wiki/Dubai_School_of_Government"

ENGECON Dubai

The **Dubai Branch of Saint Petersburg State University of Engineering and Economics** is the first branch to be established outside Russia and also is known as **ENGECON Dubai** (Russian: *ИНЖЭКОН Дубай*).

Source (edited): "http://en.wikipedia.org/wiki/ENGECON_Dubai"

Heriot-Watt University Dubai

Heriot-Watt University Dubai is a campus of the Scottish Heriot-Watt University in the city of Dubai, United Arab Emirates. The Dubai Campus, located in Dubai International Academic City offers a quality British education to students and executives from around the Gulf and further afield. Heriot-Watt University is the eighth oldest higher education institution in the United Kingdom, with a main campus in Edinburgh and further campuses in Galashiels, Orkney, and now in Dubai.

Set in a purpose-built campus of over 40,000 sq ft (3,700 m). the Dubai campus of Heriot-Watt University offers various programmes in Management, Engineering, Construction and Information Technology. An additional course in Engineering will also be introduced in the near future.

Source (edited): "http://en.wikipedia.org/wiki/Heriot-Watt_University_Dubai"

Hogeschool-Universiteit Brussel

Hogeschool-Universiteit Brussel (HUBrussel or HUB) is a European university which was founded in 2007. The HUBrussel is the result of the merger between Brussels-based colleges European University College Brussels, VLEKHO, HONIM and the Catholic University of Brussels (KUBrussel).

HUBrussel offers degrees both on university and university college level in Flanders, the Dutch-speaking (northern) region of Belgium. Building on eight decades of experience in business education, the institute provides a tradition of innovative, high-level, business-oriented education. Degrees are offered both in Dutch and in English.

History

European University College Brussels (EHSAL) was founded in 1925 and was one of the first European business colleges to obtain the ISO 9001 certificate (in 1996) for its outstanding academic quality and excellent service to its students.

In 2008, after the merger with VLEKHO, HONIM and KUBrussel, more than 9,000 students are attending classes in undergraduate, graduate and academic advanced programmes at seven faculties. HUBrussel had five faculties in Brussels, one in Dilbeek and one in Dubai.

HUBrussel is member of the Catholic University of Leuven Association, one of the oldest and most respected universities in Europe.

Programs

HUBrussel programmes are organised by two educational divisions

Academic Bachelors and Masters

The academic Bachelors and Masters are based around 3 faculties that together offer 13 undergraduate and graduate programmes:
- Economics and Management:
Commercial Sciences
Commercial Engineering
Environment, Health & Safety Management
- Linguistics and Literature:
Literature
Applied Linguistics
Interpretation, Translation
Multilingual Communication
Journalism
- Law

Professional Bachelors

The professional Bachelors include 4 fields of study that offer 13 undergraduate programmes:
- Education:
Nursery Teaching
Primary Education
Secondary Education
- Health Care:
Occupational Therapy
Medical Imaging
Nursing
Optics & Optometry
- Social and Community Work:
Social Work
Socio-educational Care Work
Family Sciences
- Commercial Sciences and Management
Operations Management
Office Management
Applied Informatics

Figures

- The number of participants in postgraduate programmes and seminars amounts to 9500
- Over 500 regular non-EU students in degree programmes in Brussels (appr. 120 annually in Dubai)
- Over 100 regular (non-Belgian) EU students in degree programmes in Brussels
- Appr. 170 inbound exchange students and 110 outbound exchange students
- Number of staff: 1100

Source (edited): "http://en.wikipedia.org/wiki/Hogeschool-Universiteit_Brussel"

Institute of Islamic and Arabic Studies (Dubai)

The **Islamic and Arabic Studies College Dubai** operates programs aimed at foreign students, including non-Muslims. Instruction is offered in Arabic, French and English.

Source (edited): "http://en.wikipedia.org/wiki/Institute_of_Islamic_and_Arabic_Studies_(Dubai)"

Institute of Management Technology, Dubai

The Institute of Management Technology in Dubai is a newly established center, situated at the Academic city, Dubai. It is aimed at fulfilling the needs of students for a high-quality, international education.

It has a modern campus built up with all world class amenities. The institute offers hostel and transport facilities.

The lush green 17-acre (69,000 m) Wi-fi campus is meticulously designed to conform to world standards. The campus provides top-of-the-line infrastructure with state-of-the-art technology.

The Dubai campus is the third campus of IMT.

Presently 3 courses are being offered

from this campus -
- MBA (Full Time)
- Executive MBA (Full Time)
- Executive MBA (Part Time)

All the courses are duly licensed by Ministry of Higher Education, Government of U.A.E.

Classes commenced from September 2006.

Source (edited): "http://en.wikipedia.org/wiki/Institute_of_Management_Technology,_Dubai"

Institute of Management Technology, Ghaziabad

Institute of Management Technology (IMT) is one of the Top 10 B schools in India.

History

IMT was established in 1980 by eminent industrialist Shri Mahendra Nath with Dr. C. B. Gupta.

Courses

IMT offers following programmes:

Location of IMT business schools

- Two-year Post Graduate Diploma in Management
  - Post Graduate Diploma in Management - Dual Country Program (DCP)
  - Post Graduate Diploma in Management - Marketing (also known as PGDM-FT)
  - Post Graduate Diploma in Management - Human Resource
  - Post Graduate Diploma in Management - Finance
  - Post Graduate Diploma in Management - International Business
  - Post Graduate Diploma in Management - Executive
  - Post Graduate Diploma in Management - Part-Time
  - Post Graduate Diploma in Management - Information Technology
- Three-year part time MBA programme
- Doctoral programme (Ph.D.) in Management
- Management Development Programme for Executives
  - General Management Programme for Executives (GMPE)

PGDM is the oldest programme. IMT also caters to the needs of business executives through its three-year part-time postgraduate programme (PGDM P/T). Corporate participants can enroll in the Management Development Programme (MDP) to enhance their business skills and learn managerial decision making. IMT's Fellow Program in Management (FPM) programme provides doctoral-level education in business management and related disciplines.

To cater to the needs of international business managers, IMT has a Post Graduate Diploma in Business Management - International Business (PGDM-IB) programme.

Distance learning (DLP) and E-learning programmes of IMT are designed for students who are unable to take up a full- or part-time MBA courses.

IMT also undertakes national and international projects that cater to governments, corporations and other organizations.

While the Ghaziabad Campus offers all the courses, the Nagpur and Dubai campuses offer a selection of the above courses.

Accreditation

IMT's educational programmes have been recognized by All India Council for Technical Education (AICTE) and Ministry of Human Resource Development, Government of India

Admissions

Prospective students are required to qualify by taking the CAT and, after that, a group discussion and an interview.

Faculty

IMT currently has around 50 core faculty. Students play a role in faculty selection. There is a strong feedback system where students give feedback for the faculty, two times per term. The faculty is removed from the institute after bad feedback on very short notice.

Apart from permanent faculty, IMT has visiting faculty from industry and other academic institutions. Around 35 visiting faculty are associated with IMT.

Campuses

IMT has three campuses: The first one is in Ghaziabad (established in 1980); the second campus is in Nagpur (established in 2004); and a third campus in Dubai (established in 2006).

IMT Nagpur has been conceptualized as a centre for corporate excellence. The IMT Dubai campus is primarily for international education.

Academic block, IMT Ghaziabad

Ghaziabad Campus

The Ghaziabad campus is a 14.7 acre fully residential campus and is the primary campus of IMT. It was established in 1980. It presently offers PGDBM and PGDCA courses through its state-of-the-art education facilities. All the students are housed in 10 hostels.

This campus has many "Centres of Excellence" like the Centre for Global Supply Chain Management.

The Ghaziabad campus infrastructure consists of academic blocks; student hostels; combined mess, canteens and Nescafe stall; amphitheatrel; MDP block and guest house; car and bike parking; lush green field and well-equipped library. A football field, a badminton and tennis court, a floodlit volleyball court, a floodlit basketball court, a floodlit tennis court, jogging tracks and a multipurpose gymnasium are some of the key recreational features of the campus.

This being the primary campus, it offers all the programmes of IMT.

Nagpur Campus

Main Building, IMT Nagpur

The Nagpur campus spans an area of 25 acres, has a completely Wi-Fi campus with state of the art facilities, and offers PGDBM in various disciplines (Marketing/Finance/HR/IT/Operations, etc.). It has a lush green environment and is equipped with modern infrastructure and a well-equipped hostel.

The first batch of students graduated in 2006 and were well placed in premier companies.

Dubai Campus

Main Building, IMT Dubai

The newly established center is situated in the Academic City, Dubai. It has a modern campus built up with all world-class amenities. The institute offers hostel and transport facilities.

The lush green 17-acre (69,000 m) Wi-fi campus is designed to conform to world standards. The campus provides modern infrastructure with state-of-the-art technology.

Presently three courses are being offered from this campus:
- MBA (Full Time)
- Executive MBA (Full Time)
- Executive MBA (Part Time)

It was granted accreditation by the Commission for Academic Accreditation, Ministry of Higher Education and Scientific Research, UAE in September 2007. It is the only Business School of Indian origin to be so accredited.

The part-time MBA course is conducted in the evenings for 18 months.

Admission is based on GMAT/CAT scores or a test conducted by IMT and a group discussion, interview and academic records, he said.

The first batch commenced from September 2006.

Events

The constant interaction with the corporate sector is done through:
- Shrinkhla, a series of seminars on various important issues facing the industry
- Synergies, a series of round table conferences of industry heads
- Compass, an annual consultancy symposium
- Conquest, a series of live short-term projects in the area of HR

Other competitions are also organized. A few of them are:
- Chakravyuh, B-school sports festival at IMT, Ghaziabad
- Tatva, Inter B-School Summer Internship Presentation Contest, at IMT, Ghaziabad
- Passion is the annual B-school fest of IMT, Ghaziabad
- Marketing World Cup is the Annual Inter B-school Marketing Competition at IMT Ghaziabad
- Milestone 35 is the annual B-school fest of IMT, Nagpur

Placements

Placements are usually conducted on the first Sunday of January. Over the years, IMT, Ghaziabad has always maintained an impeccable 100% placement record.

Rating

IMT Ghaziabad has consistently been ranked among the top 10 business schools in India. IMT Ghaziabad has been ranked as the third best private B-school in India according to the Mint's Best B-schools Survey 2008. IMT Ghaziabad belongs to the Super League, i.e., in the Top 7 category of the top business schools in India as surveyed by AIMA - IMRB Survey (All India Management Association).

Notable alumni

A few of the notable alumni are:
- Rajeev Karwal, founder and CEO, Milagrow Business & Knowledge Solutions, ex-CEO of Electrolux Kelvinator India, ex- Chief Executive, Consumer Durables, Reliance Retail
- Prasoon Joshi, eminent advertising personality and regional creative director, APAC, McCann Erickson
- Mini Mathur, *Indian Idol* hostess on Sony TV, ex-MTV VJ
- Nitish Katara, business executive who was a victim of an honour killing
- Sachin Pilot, youngest MP from Congress Party
- Pranava Prakash, artist

Gallery

IMT Ghaziabad

Academic Block, IMT Ghaziabad

Amphitheatre, IMT Ghaziabad

Hostel complex, IMT Ghaziabad

Library, IMT Ghaziabad

IMT Nagpur

Academic Block, IMT Nagpur

Front Gate, IMT Nagpur

Hostel block, IMT Nagpur

Main block, IMT Nagpur

IMT Nagpur

IMT Nagpur

IMT Dubai

IMT Dubai

IMT Dubai

Source (edited): "http://en.wikipedia.org/wiki/Institute_of_Management_Technology,_Ghaziabad"

List of universities and colleges in Dubai

There are sizable numbers of **universities and colleges in Dubai**. Dubai's educational institutions include public and private universities and colleges.

List of public universities and colleges
- Higher Colleges of Technology
- Zayed University
- Dubai Medical College for Girls

List of private universities and colleges
- Centre for Executive Education, Dubai Knowledge Village
- London Human Resources Institute, Dubai Centre, Knowledge Village
- Hult International Business School
- Islamic Azad University, Dubai
- Shahid Beheshti University, Dubai
- RIT Dubai
- Cass Business School
- London Business School
- Heriot Watt University
- Al Ghurair University
- Dubai School of Government
- American College of Dubai
- Skyline University College
- American University in Dubai
- British University in Dubai
- Canadian University Of Dubai
- Manchester University Business School
- Allied Institute of Management Studies (AIMS), Dubai Knowledge Village
- Dubai University College
- European University College Brussels (Hogeschool-Universiteit Brussel)
- Mahatma Gandhi University
- MAHE-Manipal
- HAwowid
- SAE Institute
- Birla Institute of Technology & Science, Pilani - Dubai
- University of Wollongong in Dubai
- S.P.Jain Center Of Management, Dubai
- Institute of Management Technology, Dubai
- The Emirates Academy of Hospitality Management
- Murdoch University International Study Centre Dubai
- Emirates Aviation College
- Boston University Dental School
- Dubai Medical College for Girls
- University of Dubai
- University of Waterloo
- Islamic & Arabic Studies College Dubai
- Middlesex University - Dubai Campus
- Universal Empire Institute of Medical Sciences
- SZABIST (Shaheed Zulfikar Ali Bhutto Institute of Science and Technology)

Source (edited): "http://en.wikipedia.org/wiki/List_of_universities_and_colleges_in_Dubai"

Mahatma Gandhi University

Mahatma Gandhi University, also known as **M G University**, was established on 2 October 1983 in Kottayam. The University Grants Commission of India does not believe that the names of Indian universities should be unique, so another UGC-recognized government-run Mahatma Gandhi University was established in 2007 in Andhra Pradesh; and was not challenged by the older Mahatma Gandhi University. The older Mahatma Gandhi University (formerly Gandhiji University), has been accredited (B+) by the National Assessment and Accreditation Council, India. The next visit takes place between Nov 24 and 27, 2011. The University has 223 affiliated colleges spread over five districts in central Kerala. University offers various academic programmes in the fields of Gandhian Thought, International Relations&Politics, Technology, Physics, Nano Science, Disability Studies and Rehabilitation Sciences, Special Education and Rehabilitation Sciences, Rehabilitation Psychology, Behavioural Medicine and Rehabilitation, Rehabilitation Nursing, Journalism, Chemical Sciences including Polymer Chemistry, Nursing, Hospital Administration, Environmental Sciences and Disaster Management among others. Currently Dr. P. M. Rajan Gurukkal is the Vice Chancellor and Prof. Rajan Varughese is the Pro- Vice- Chancellor.Prof. M.R. Unni is the Registrar. Dr. Thomas John Mapra holds the charge of Contorller of Examinations. Abraham J Puthumana is the Finance Officer, Prof. P.P. Ravindran holds the charge of DCDC and Mr. G. Sreekumar is the Public Relations Officer.

The University is funded by the University Grants Commission and Government of Kerala. It is a member of the AIU and the ACU. Association of Commonwealth Universities represents over 480 universities from Commonwealth countries.

The University enrolls 1,50,000 students on an average every year to 210 Courses in graduate, post graduate and M.Phil/Ph.D. programmes through various departments and colleges.

The students have been consistently contributing to the image of the University through their outstanding performance in NSS, NCC, Inter University Youth Festivals, Sports, Games and Intellectual pursuits.

Key Features

The University teaching departments focus on research rooted in inter disciplinary frame work.

- The University has awarded approximately 1250 doctoral degrees (till 2009) for the research activities undertaken by the scholars in various disciplines. Online Access to these doctoral theses are available at www.mgutheses.org . The University has published over 5000 papers in research journals of international repute. Most of the research papers are also provided online by the University Library
- This university pioneered the total literacy campaign in Kerala(India) with their project in Kottayam(Kottayam was the first district in India to have achieved 100% literacy).
- It operates out of 8 global locations(Other than in Kerala and in other states of India).

Location

The University campus is located at the Priyadarsini Hills which is 13 Kilometers away from Kottayam Railway Station and 4 Kilometers away from Ettumannoor. In order to reach the campus one should take deviation from Ettumannor or Gandhi Nagar (from M. C. Road). The nearest airport is at Cochin which is about 80 km away. Private buses to Ernakulam starting from the Nagampadom bus stand right at the northern end of the railway platform at Kottayam stop at the University. The travel time is around 40 minutes, and the ticket costs Rs.7.00 (15 euro cents) Autorickshas ply the distance for about Rs.150 (about 3 euros).

Mahatma Gandhi University has made its presence outside its territorial jurisdiction through the 72 off campus centres – 55 centres within Kerala, 9 outside Kerala and at 8 global locations.

University Teaching Departments

- Dept. of life long learning & extension
- Behavioural Science,School Of
- Bio science,School Of
- Chemical Science,School Of
- Computer Science,School Of
- Distance education,School Of
- Environmental Science,School Of
- Gandhian thought and development studies,School Of
- Indian legal thought,School Of
- International relation & politics,School Of
- Printing & publishing,School Of
- Letters,School Of
- Pedagogical sciences,School Of
- Physical education & sports science,School Of
- Pure and applied physics,School Of
- Management & business studies,School Of
- Social science,School Of
- Tourism studies,School Of

Affiliated Colleges

Among the prominent affiliated colleges(more than 183 colleges) are

- Amal Jyothi College
- Athurasrammam N.S.S Homeo College
- Baselius College
- Bishop Abraham Memorial College, Thurithicadu
- Bishop Kurialacherry College for Women
- CMS College Kottayam
- Caarmel Engineering College, Perunad, Pathanamthitta.
- College of Applied Science (IHRD), Kattappana
- Ettumanoorappan College, Ettumanoor
- Federal Institute of Science And Technology, Angamaly
- Kuriakose Gregarios college
- M.E.S College, Marampally
- Mar Augusthinose College
- Mar Thoma College, Thiruvalla
- Mount Carmel Training College
- [Nirmala College, Muvattupuzha]
- N.S.S college, Changanassery
- N.S.S Training College, Changanassery
- Medical college, Kottayam
- Mount Zion College of Engineering Kadammanitta
- Marian college ,Kuttikkanam,Idukki

[http://mathacollegeoftechnology.edu.in
- Matha College Of Technology, Manakkappadi, North Paravur, Ernakulam]
- Government College Manimalakunnu
- School of Technology and Applied Sciences
- SCMS School of Engineering and Technology, Ernakulam
- Pavanatma College, Murrickacherry
- Mangalam College of Education
- RLV College of Music and Fine Arts, Tripunithura
- st.George's college, Aruvithura
- St Johns College Of Nursing, Kattappana
- St.Teresa's college, Ernakulam
- Sacred Hearts college, Tevara
- S A S SNDP YOGAM College, Konni
- S. B. College
- S.N.M training College, Moothakunnam
- S.N.M College, Maliyankara, Moothakunnan
- St. Albert's college, Ernakulam
- St. Xavier's College
- St. Josephs Training College
- St.Joseph's college of engineering & technology, Palai
- St. Mary's College
- St. Stephen's College
- St. Thomas College, PALA
- Sree Vidyadhi Raja N S S College
- St. Thomas Training College
- St. Johns Institute of Technology, Pathanamthitta
- Union Christian College, Aluva
- St. Dominic's College, Kanjirapally
- The Cochin College, Cochin
- Viswajyothi College of Engineering and Technology, Vazhakulam
- K.M.E.A College of Engineering and Technology

Source (edited): "http://en.wikipedia.org/wiki/Mahatma_Gandhi_University"

Rochester Institute of Technology, Dubai

RIT Dubai is a satellite campus of Rochester Institute of Technology, New York, USA in Dubai, United Arab Emirates. The college, is located in the Dubai Silicon Oasis, The campus started offering post graduate courses in Fall 2008. In 2009, there are plans to offer a full-time graduate program, and in 2010, a full-time undergraduate program. By 2019, RIT plans to expand the campus to 1,000,000 square feet (93,000 m), accepting around 4,000 students.

Since RIT already has campuses in Croatia and Kosovo, the Dubai campus will give RIT students cooperative education opportunities in another country.

Programs Offered

Undergraduate Programs
- Applied Arts and Sciences
- Business and Management
- Management
- Marketing
- Management Information Systems
- International Business
- Computing and Information Sciences
- Information Technology
- Applied Networking
- Information Security and Forensics
- Engineering
- Electrical Engineering
- Mechanical Engineering

Graduate Programs
- Master of Business Administration
- Masters of Engineering
- Mechanical Engineering
- Masters of Science
- Finance
- Electrical Engineering
- Service Leadership and Innovation
- Networking and Systems Administration
- Human Resource Development

Advanced Graduate Certificates
- Computer Security and Information Assurance
- Service Leadership and Innovation
- Project Management

Source (edited): "http://en.wikipedia.org/wiki/Rochester_Institute_of_Technology,_Dubai"

Shaheed Zulfiqar Ali Bhutto Institute of Science and Technology

Shaheed Zulfikar Ali Bhutto Institute of Science and Technology (commonly referred to as SZABIST), is a Pakistani university, with headquarters at Karachi and campuses at Islamabad, Karachi, Larkana and Dubai. The institute offers programs in Business Administration, Computer Science, Media Sciences, Social Sciences, Law and Development Economics, Engineering (Mechatronics). SZABIST has been ranked at No.3 in Business/I.T category by Higher Education Commission (HEC)

Established through an Act of Sindh Assembly (Sindh Act No. XI of 1995) and is approved and recognized by the Higher Education Commission (HEC) as a degree granting institution. SZABIST has campuses in Karachi, Islamabad, Larkana & Dubai. It is a registered member of the International Association of Universities (IAU), Association of Commonwealth Universities (ACU), Federation of the Universities of the Islamic World (FUIW), Asia University Federation (AUF) and the Association of SAARC Universities (ASU).

Programs offered

The school offers programs in management sciences, computer sciences, me-

dia sciences, law, economics and social sciences. Some of the programs offered are external programs offered in collaboration with universities in the UK. Following is a list of offered degrees:
- Management Sciences

Bachelor of Business Administration (BBA), Master of Business Administration (MBA), Master of Science (MS) in Management Sciences and Doctor of Philosophy (PhD) in Management Sciences.
- Computer Sciences

Bachelor of Science (BS) in Computer Sciences, Master of Science (MS) in Computer Sciences, Doctor of Philosophy (PhD) in Computer Sciences.
- BE Mechatronics Engineering

Bachelor of Engineering (BE) in Mechatronics Engineering
- Social Sciences

Bachelor of Science (BSc) in Media Studies, Bachelor of Sciences (BS) in Social Sciences and Economics, Master of Science (MS) in Social Sciences & Economics and Doctor of Philosophy (PhD) in Social Sciences & Economics.
- External Programs

Zulfiqar Ali Bhutto Institute of Science and Technology offers external programs in Law (LLB) and Economics & Development (BSc) in collaboration with the University of London.
Intermediate program:
SZABIST offers Intermediate at SZABIST INTERMEDIATE LARKANA.IN AFFILIATION WITH BISE LARKANA.

Faculty

Shaheed Zulfiqar Ali Bhutto Institute of Science and Technology past and present faculty includes Javaid Laghari and Kaiser Bengali.

Alumni

Source (edited): "http://en.wikipedia.org/wiki/Shaheed_Zulfiqar_Ali_Bhutto_Institute_of_Science_and_Technology"

Tamkeen

Tamkeen is Arabic for enablement and empowerment. **Tamkeen Group** based in Saudi Arabia is a leading industrial and trading company that markets its products and services across the Middle East.

In the UAE **Tamkeen** is a center that is established by the government of Dubai to help people with vision impairment problems get hold of the latest advances in the IT field and acquire other skills that they need for the labour market. The centre was opened in March 2004. The number of graduates from the centre has grown to 24 in 2005. The centre will then find those graduates appropriate jobs. Only one graduate has worked in DIfc.
Source (edited): "http://en.wikipedia.org/wiki/Tamkeen"

The Emirates Academy of Hospitality Management

The Emirates Academy of Hospitality Management is an educational institution in Dubai, United Arab Emirates. Established in 2001 by the Jumeirah Group, it is the first major academy focusing on tourism and hospitality education at the university level in the Middle East.

History

Since its inception on 5 October 2001, The Emirates Academy of Hospitality Management has been meticulously planned to fulfill the exacting requirements of tourism and hospitality management education.

His Highness Sheikh Mohammed bin Rashid Al Maktoum, Vice-President and Prime Minister of the UAE and Ruler of Dubai, is the owner of Jumeirah and the Academy's patron.

Campus

The Emirates Academy of Hospitality Management's campus provides students a safe, comfortable and dynamic environment conducive to learning, hard work and interaction. Sports and leisure facilities are shared with management employees of Jumeirah, offering students the opportunity to interact with industry professionals on a daily basis.

An optional academic year at the École hôtelière de Lausanne in Switzerland is available to students in the Bachelor's program.

Academic profile

The Ministry of Higher Education and Scientific Research for the United Arab Emirates licenses and accredits The Emirates Academy of Hospitality Management and its degree courses. The Emirates Academy of Hospitality Management offers students two main courses of study:
- Bachelor of Science Degree with Honours in International Hospitality Management
- Associate Degree in International Hospitality Operations

A Master of Science degree program is currently under development.
Source (edited): "http://en.wikipedia.org/wiki/The_Emirates_Academy_of_Hospitality_Management"

University of Dubai

The **University of Dubai** (**UD**) is an accredited university in the UAE with a focus community, innovation and diversity. The University of Dubai degree programs are recognized by the Ministry of Higher Education & Scientific Research (MOHESR) in the UAE, as well as the international accreditation bodies in the world including AACSB accreditation for the College of Business Administration, and CAC-ABET accreditation for the Computing and Information Systems program.

History

The University of Dubai was established in 1997 by the Dubai Chamber of Commerce and Industry (DC) to address skills and qualifications gaps in the workforce and to support the government's human resources development programs in the private and public sectors..

Campus

The University of Dubai's current Downtown Campus is situated in the center of Dubai with some classes held in the Dubai Chamber in Diera, Dubai.

In June 2006 His Highness Sheikh Mohammed Bin Rashid Al Maktoum, Vice President and Prime Minister of the UAE and Ruler of Dubai, kindly granted the university 3,000,000 square feet (280,000 m) of land in Academic City for construction of new state-of-the-art campus.

Academics

College of Business Administration (CBA)

The University Of Dubai's College of Business Administration (CBA) is accredited locally in the UAE by the Ministry of higher Education & Scientific Research (MOHESR/CAA) and internationally by the Association to Advance Collegiate Schools of Business (AACSB).

The University of Dubai's College of Business Administration (CBA) offers BBA degree in eight different majors: Management, Marketing, Finance and Banking, Accounting, Human Resources Management, Entrepreneurship Management, Business Economics and Supply Chain and Logistics Management.

College of Information Technology (CIT)

The University Of Dubai's College of Information Technology offers a Computing and Information Systems (CIS) program which is accredited locally in the UAE by the Ministry of Higher Education & Scientific Research (MOHESR) and internationally by the Computing Accreditation Commission (CAC) of the Accreditation Board for Engineering and Technology (ABET) in USA.

Masters of Business Administration (MBA)

The University of Dubai offers a MBA through the College of Business Administration. The University of Dubai MBA Program is designed to prepare business leaders and professionals for successful careers in organizations as it enhances critical thinking, increases oral and written communication skills, builds appreciation for diverse cultural perspectives, improves decision making in a rapidly changing global environment and reinforces the application of knowledge and skills in problem solving. Ethics and corporate social responsibility are woven throughout the curriculum.

The MBA Program is designed with four double concentrations in order to meet the needs of professionals in these areas

These Double Concentrations are: Leadership & Human Resource Management (LHRM); Logistics & Operations Management (LOM); Accounting & Finance (AF) and International Business & Marketing (IBM)

Accreditation

The University of Dubai is accredited by:

- The UAE Ministry of Higher Education and Scientific Research
- The AACSB International Accreditation
- CIS program accredited by the Computing Accreditation Commission ABET, Inc.

Scholarships for government organizations

University of Dubai offers two full scholarships (covering tuition fees) for each governmental Authority/Department tied to the Government of Dubai. The Authority/Department chooses two candidates with the only condition that they are UAE nationals.

Student services

The University of Dubai's Department of Student Services (DSS) provides a variety of programs and services including counseling, student life, academic advising, dining, transportation, and health services.

Governance and support of Dubai Chamber of Commerce and Industry

University of Dubai receives its authority and funding support from the Dubai Chamber of Commerce and Industry. The Ruler's Court of Dubai appoints the Board of Directors of Dubai Chamber of Commerce and Industry.

The Board of Trustees of University of Dubai is drawn from the Dubai Chamber of Commerce and Industry Board of Directors. The University of Dubai Board of Trustees has the responsibility for determining the strategic objectives and necessary funding of the University. It considers and monitors proposals from University of Dubai for all aspects of strategy, academic portfolios, development, policy making, regulations and funding to support students and staff.

Source (edited): "http://en.wikipedia.org/wiki/University_of_Dubai"

Fujairah College

Fujairah College (FC) is a higher education institution in the city of Fujairah, United Arab Emirates.

The foundation of the college was initiated by the members of the Fujairah Welfare Association (FWA). It is a semi-governmental and non-profit making educational institution. FC was formally established in April 2006 and its programmes are accredited by the Commission for Academic Accreditation, a department of the Ministry of Higher Education and Scientific Research.

The Board of Trustees includes His Excellency Saed Ben Muhammad Al-Raqabani and His Excellency Hameed Al-Gatamy. The Chief Executive Officer is Dr Ghassan Al-Qaimairi. The first two associate degrees offered from 1 September 2006 were in Business Administration and Information Technology.

There are plans for a campus. Meanwhile, the College has been using the Fujairah Trade Center (FTC), especially floors 10–12.

Source (edited): "http://en.wikipedia.org/wiki/Fujairah_College"

George Mason University

George Mason University (often referred to as **GMU** or **Mason**) is a public university based in unincorporated Fairfax County, Virginia, United States, south of and adjacent to the city of Fairfax. Additional campuses are located nearby in Arlington County, Prince William County, and Loudoun County. The university's motto is *Freedom and Learning* while its slogan or tagline is *Where Innovation Is Tradition*.

Named after American revolutionary, patriot, and founding father George Mason, the university was founded as a branch of the University of Virginia in 1957 and became an independent institution in 1972. Today, Mason is recognized for its strong programs in economics, law, creative writing, and computer science. In recent years, George Mason's department of economics has twice won the Nobel Prize in Economics. The university enrolls over 32,500 students, making it the largest university by head count in the Commonwealth of Virginia.

History

The Virginia General Assembly passed a resolution in January 1956, establishing a branch college of the University of Virginia in Northern Virginia. In September 1957 the new college opened its doors to seventeen students, all of whom enrolled as freshmen in a renovated elementary school building at Bailey's Crossroads. John Norville Gibson Finley served as Director of the new branch, which was known as University College.

George Mason, (1725–1792) after whom the University is named.

The city of Fairfax purchased and donated 150 acres (0.61 km) of land to the University of Virginia for the college's new site, which was referred to as the Fairfax Campus. In 1959, the Board of Visitors of UVA selected a permanent name for the college: George Mason College of the University of Virginia. The Fairfax campus construction planning that began in early 1960 showed visible results when the development of the first 40 acres (160,000 m) of Fairfax Campus began in 1962. In the Fall of 1964 the new campus welcomed 356 students.

Local jurisdictions of Fairfax County, Arlington County, and the cities of Alexandria and Falls Church agreed to appropriate $3 million to purchase land adjacent to Mason to provide for a 600-acre (2.4 km) Fairfax Campus in 1966 with the intention that the institution would expand into a regional university of major proportions, including the granting of graduate degrees.

On April 7, 1972 the Virginia General Assembly enacted legislation which separated George Mason College from its parent institution, the University of Virginia. Renamed that day by the legislation, George Mason College became George Mason University.

In 1978, the George Mason University Foundation purchased the former Kann's department store in Arlington. In March 1979 the Virginia General Assembly authorized the establishment of the George Mason University School of Law (GMUSL) – contingent on the transfer of the Kann's building to George Mason University. GMUSL began operations in that building on July 1, 1979 and received provisional accreditation from the American Bar Association in 1980. The ABA granted full approval to GMUSL in 1986.

Also, in 1979, the university moved all of its athletic programs to NCAA Division I. Enrollment that year passed 11,000. The university opened its Arlington campus in 1982, two blocks from the Virginia Square-GMU station in Arlington. In 1986 the university's governing body, the Board of Visitors, approved a new master plan for the year based on an enrollment of 20,000 full-time students with housing for 5,000 students by 1995. That same year university housing opened to bring the total number of residential students to 700.

Through a bequest of Russian immigrant Shelley Krasnow the University established the Krasnow Institute for Advanced Study in 1991. The Institute was created to further the understanding of the mind and intelligence by combining the fields of cognitive psychology, neurobiology, and artificial intelligence. In 1992, Mason's new Prince William Institute began classes in a temporary site in Manassas, Virginia. The Institute moved to a permanent 124-acre (0.50 km) site located on the Rt. 234 bypass, ten miles (16 km) south of Manassas, by the year 1997, and is now known as the Prince William Campus. The university graduated more than 5,000 students that following spring.

While George Mason University is young compared to established research universities in Virginia, it has grown rapidly, reaching an enrollment of 30,714 students in 2008. According to a 2005 report issued by the university, enrollment is expected to reach 35,000 students by 2011 with more than 7,000 resident students.

In 2002, Mason celebrated its 30th anniversary as a university by launching its first capital campaign, trying to raise $110 million. The school raised $142 million, $32 million more than its goal. The George Mason University logo, originally designed in 1982, was updated in 2004.

In 2008, the School of Management celebrated its 30th anniversary. Also, in 2008 Mason changed its mascot from the "Gunston" animal to the "Patriot".

Fairfax Campus

The new Volgenau School of Information Technology and Engineering building.

The main campus of George Mason University is situated on 677 acres (2.74 km) just south of the City of Fairfax, Virginia in central Fairfax County, approximately 15 miles (24 km) west of Washington, D.C.

The Fairfax campus is served on the Washington Metro by the Vienna/Fairfax-GMU station on the Orange line. A 15 minute shuttle in addition to the CUE bus, free for students with a Mason ID card, serves the students through routes from the Metro station to the University.

Design and construction

In the early 1960s four buildings were constructed around a lawn in Fairfax, appropriately named East, West, North (later, Krug Hall), and South (later, Finley Hall). The first four structures, today dubbed "The Original Four," "around a lawn" were understood as a clear reference to the buildings around The Lawn of the University of Virginia in Charlottesville. In addition, in the words of the architects, the architecture of the buildings was meant to reflect Jeffersonian influence through the use of red brick with buff colored mortar, white vertical columns, and sloped shingled roofs.

Master plans were developed to incorporate further development, which saw new additions such as Fenwick Library and Lecture Hall. By 1979 master plan development was handled by the firm of Sasaki & Associates, which continued to work alongside the university in the years that followed. Student housing first became available in 1977. The 1980s saw the university expand with a new building being added on each year, including the Patriot Center. As well as the construction of the Fairfax campuses network of hot and cold water piping that provides power efficient, centralized heating and cooling for the university's buildings.

Recent years have once again brought a new construction boom to the Fairfax campus, which is currently undergoing a massive, $900 million construction campaign (between 2002–2012). This has brought about a huge influx of new buildings to campus, and renovations of existing buildings, most recently:

Building Name / Type / Description - Completion Date

- Southside - New - All you can eat style dinning hall - Fall 2008
- Recreation and Athletic Complex [RAC] - Renovated/Expanded - Fall 2009
- Hampton Roads - New - Student Housing for ~400 students in suite-style single and double occupancy rooms and feature lounges and study spaces on each floor) - Fall 2010
- Pilot House - New - Late night dinner open from 10pm to 4am - Fall 2010
- Student Union I [SUB I] - Renovated/Expanded - Fall 2011
- Student Union II [SUB II] - Renovated - Spring 2011
- Student Housing VIII [temporary name] - Under Construction - Spring 2012
- Thompson & Pohick - Under Renovation - Fall 2011
- Science & Technology II Renovation/Expansion - Under Renovation/Construction - 2013

Not only is Mason experiencing a construction boom, but it also has another Master Plan and Library Master Plan in the works with plans with a focus on energy efficiency. January 2009 GMU installed LED lighting throughout the Fairfax Campus. This compliments Mason's existing comprehensive building automation system, which links all buildings to the Facilities Management Energy Management Office, who automatically regulate the heating, cooling and lighting systems of buildings across the Fairfax campus.

Housing and residence life

Fairfax is the only campus of George Mason University with on-campus student and grad student housing. The campus is divided up into three neighborhoods, which combine house approximately 5,000 students. A seventh housing area is currently under construction to house an additional 600 students and more dining facilities.

Southeast:

Liberty Square, an upperclassmen residence area which opened in 2003

- Liberty Square - Upperclassmen - Completed 2003, and housing approximately 500 students in two and four person apartments. Each apartment is fully furnished, and contains a kitchen and living/dining area.
- Potomac Heights - Upperclassmen - Completed 2004, and housing approximately 500 students in apartments which can accommodate two, four or six students in single and double bedrooms. Each apartment is fully furnished, and contains a kitchen and living/dining area.
- Presidents Park - Freshmen - Completed in 1989, and housing approximately 1,100 students in twelve halls (Adams, Kennedy, Roosevelt, Harrison, Lincoln, Truman, Jackson, Madison, Wilson, Jefferson, Monroe, Washington). All rooms are fully furnished and residents reside in double, triple, or quad rooms and use shared common bathrooms cleaned daily by janitorial staff. By Fall 2011 all halls will have been renovated within the last 4 years. The twelve resident halls surround Eisenhower hall in the center, a non-residential building which contains a late night diner called Ike's (open until 4am), a large study lounge, a handful of small group study rooms, HDTV lounge with a pool table and vending machines.

Central:

A view of George Mason's Chesapeake housing area.

- Chesapeake - Upperclassmen - Completed 2004, and housing approximately 800 students among its 4 halls (Blue Ridge, Shenandoah, Piedmont, Tidewater) in suite-style apartments for four people which vary in combining single and double bedrooms, all which share a common bathroom. Each apartment is fully furnished, and each floor of every building contains at least two large study rooms (in some cases three). Blue Ridge currently houses the One Stop Patriot Shop convent store on it's lower level. Additionally, Tidewater is the future location of GMU's very own Red Mango and Auntie Anne's, opening Fall 2011.
- Dominion - Upperclassmen - Completed in 1981, and housing approximately 500 students in suite-style double occupancy rooms, which share bathrooms with the adjacent suite. All rooms are fully furnished and each floor contains a single study lounge. Renovations are currently being planned.
- Eastern Shore - Freshmen Honors School Students - Completed in 2009, and housing approximately 200 students in suite-style rooms holding up to four residents sharing a single bathroom. Each cluster of 16 students has access to a common living room, kitchen and study space.
- University Commons - Freshmen - Completed in 1986, and housing approximately 500 students in seven halls (Amherst, Brunswick, Carroll, Dickenson, Essex, Franklin, and Grayson). All rooms are fully furnished and residents reside in single, double, or triple rooms and use shared common bathrooms cleaned daily by janitorial staff. Renovations are currently scheduled to take place in phases, and will be completed by 2013.

Northwest:

- Commonwealth - Upperclassman - Completed in 1981, and housing approximately 500 students in suite-style double occupancy rooms, which share bathrooms with the adjacent suite. All rooms are fully furnished and each floor contains a single study lounge. Renovations are currently being planned.
- Hampton Roads - All Students - Completed in 2010 and housing approximately 400 students. Hampton Roads is also home to the Pilot House (open until 4am), Mason's second on-campus late night diner.
- Northern Neck - Upperclassman - Completed in 2008 and housing approximately 400 students. Northern Neck is also home to Mason's only Starbucks, located in its first floor.
- Student Apartments - Upperclassman - Housing approximately 500 students, in bedroom apartments, each bedroom accommodating two students and each suite sharing one bathroom. Suites has between one, to three bedrooms and are fully furnished, and contains a small kitchen and combined living/dining area.
- Townhouses - Upperclassman - 35 two-bedroom townhouses located 1/8 of a mile north of the campus on State Route 123

Former Buildings:
- Patriot Village

In summer 2008 the Patriot Village area

was demolished to make room for the RAC (an on campus gym complex). Patriots Village consisted of dozens of permanent modulars located just outside of Patriot Circle, east of Ox Road, offering modular and suite-style units.

Notable Campus Buildings

Barack Obama delivering a speech to students at the Johnson Center in 2007.

Johnson Center

The George W. Johnson Learning Center, more commonly known as the Johnson Center or JC, is the central hub on campus, completed in 1995 and named after University President of 18-years, George W. Johnson. Located in the center of campus, the $30 million, 320,000-square-foot (30,000 m) building was built as the first of its kind building on any American campus, acting both as a library and a student union. The ground floor includes a buffet style restaurant named the Bistro, the campus radio station WGMU Radio, a coffee shop named Jazzman's, 300-seat movie theater, and Dewberry Hall. The main floor includes the campus bookstore, a large food court with several fast food restaurants, a patisserie and the ground floor of the library. The second and third floors of the Johnson Center are primarily used by the library, with multiple group meeting rooms, computer labs, and a full service restaurant named George's located on the third floor.

The Johnson Center serves as the center for student life with many activities and productions sponsored by Program Board and Student Government. In 2004 during the Democratic Primaries, Senator John Kerry, the eventual Democratic Nominee for President, visited George Mason University and gave a speech on the floor of the Johnson Center. In 2007, shortly after announcing on his website that he would establish a presidential exploratory committee, Senator Barack Obama gave a speech at the "Yes We Can" rally at the Johnson Center atrium. The next week he formally announced his intentions of running for president.

Center for the Arts

George Mason University's Center for the Arts.

The Center for the Arts includes a 2,000-seat Concert Hall built in 1990. The concert hall can be converted into a more intimate 800-seat theater. Most *Center for the Arts* events take place here, including operas, orchestras, ballets, and musical and theatrical performances such as Kid Cudi in 2010.

Patriot Center

The Patriot Center is a 10,000 seat arena, home court for the Men's and Women's basketball team. The Patriot Center is also host to over 100 concerts and events throughout the year, annually attracting major performers like the Ringling Bros. and Barnum & Bailey Circus.

Aquatic and Fitness Center

The 68,000-square-foot (6,300 m) Aquatic and Fitness Center opened in 1998 at a cost of $11 million. The center includes an Olympic size swimming pool containing eight 50-meter lanes, twenty-two 25-yard (23 m) lanes, two movable bulkheads, and a diving area equipped with two 1-meter and two 3-meter spring boards, a Warm-water recreational pool, Locker rooms, a whirlpool, a coed sauna, and a family changing room.

Fenwick Library

Fenwick Library

Fenwick Library was originally built in 1967, with additions in 1974, a tower in 1983, and renovations in 2005–2006. It was named for Charles Rogers Fenwick, one of George Mason's founders. Fenwick Library is the main research library at George Mason. Its resources include: most of the university's books, microfilms, print and bound journals, government documents, and maps. Electronic resources include networked and stand-alone CD-ROMs, the libraries' online catalog, a number of databases available through the libraries' membership in various consortia, and Internet access. Another important collection of research materials housed in Fenwick is the Government Documents collection. This collection includes both federal and Virginia state documents. Both sets of documents contain items from the administrative, legislative, and judicial branches of government, and constitute an invaluable source of primary source materials for students and faculty in political science, public policy, sociology, business and other fields. There is also a special GIS center in Fenwick Library which conducts GIS drop-in sessions every week.

George Mason is a member of the Consortium of Universities of the Washington Metropolitan Area, granting it access to resources of thirteen other libraries in the District of Columbia.

Arlington Campus

The George Mason University School of Law on the Arlington campus

The 5.2-acre (21,000 m) Arlington campus was established in 1979 by the Virginia General Assembly for the newly founded law school. In 1980, graduate and professional programs were also offered in the building, a converted Kann's department store. Since then the school has grown to offer a multitude of graduate degrees. In 1996, Arlington's campus began its first phase in a three phase campus redevelopment project. In 1998, Hazel Hall was completed to house the law school, the Mercatus Center, and the Institute for Humane Studies. The second phase, to be completed in 2010, is underway for a 250,000-square-foot (23,000 m) building named Founders Hall is to house the Schools of Public Policy, Education and Human Development, Information Technology, Engineering, Management, the Institute for Conflict Analysis and Resolution, Computational Science, and the College of Visual & Performing Arts and academic and student supports services. Arlington's campus is projected to reach an enrollment of 10,000 students by the completion of its redevelopment.

The Arlington campus is served on the Washington Metro by the Virginia Square-GMU station on the Orange line. The station is located approximately two blocks west of the campus.

Prince William Campus

George Mason's Prince William campus opened on August 25, 1997 in Manassas. It is located on 124 acres (0.50 km) of land. The campus offers a high-tech/bio-tech and emphasizes bioinformatics, biotechnology, forensic biosciences educational and research programs in addition to computer and information technology. The campus also offers creative programs of instruction, research, and public/private partnerships in the Prince William County area.

Prince William offers an M.A. in New Professional Studies in Teaching, an M.A.I.S. with a concentration in Recreation Resources Management, a B.S. in Administration of Justice, undergraduate programs in health, fitness, and 'Recreation Resources', graduate programs in exercise, fitness and 'Health Promotion', and nontraditional programs through continuing and professional education in geographic information systems and facility management.

Prince William also boasts the 300-seat Verizon Auditorium, the 110,000-square-foot (10,000 m) Freedom Aquatic and Fitness Center, and a 85,000-square-foot (7,900 m), $46 million Hylton Performing Arts Center which opened in 2010. Other buildings on the Prince William campus include the Occoquan Building, which houses various academic, research, and administrative resources including a Student Health clinic, Bull Run Hall, a 100,000-square-foot (9,300 m) building which opened in the fall of 2004, and Discovery Hall, which was completed in 1998 at a cost of $20.4 million.

Loudoun Campus

In the fall of 2005, the university opened a site in Loudoun County, Virginia. Several months later, it announced the gift of 123 acres (0.50 km) of land by Greenvest, LLC, to build a fourth suburban campus. The campus was scheduled to open in 2009. However, the proposal was voted down by the Loudoun County Board of Supervisors, as part of the larger Dulles South project. Greenvest rescinded the gift. Committed to expanding its presence in Loudoun, the university has now proposed a possible joint campus with Northern Virginia Community College. The campus would be located in Broadlands, Virginia.

Mason's current Loudoun site offers several graduate programs; an MA in Business Administration, Masters and doctoral programs in the College of Education and Human Development (CEHD), a graduate degree in nursing, and a Master of Science in telecommunications. The Loudon campus also offers five undergraduate programs; a minor in business and management, certificates in the College of Education and Human Development, a BS in health science, a minor in information technology, and an introductory course in social work. Other graduate level courses, such as those offered by the Department of Information and Software Engineering, are periodically taught at the site.

Ras Al Khaimah

George Mason opened a 'campus' in the Ras Al Khaimah emirate of the United Arab Emirates in 2005. No one ever graduated from the Ras al Khaimah 'campus' and it never grew beyond one building. The Ras Al Khaimah 'campus' nominally offered three undergraduate Bachelors of Science degrees in biology, business administration, and electronics and communications engineering. They subsequently added a course in "educational leadership and management."

On February 27, 2009, Mason announced they would close the Ras Al Khamimah campus at the end of the Spring 2009 semester. University Provost, Peter Stearns, cited that the relationship between George Mason University and the partner foundation in RAK worked smoothly until early 2009. He explained that the foundation would be reducing the financial support as well as attempting to change the academic reporting structure. In an e-mail to students Stearns wrote, "We have not been able to reach agreement with our RAK partner on a budget and administrative structure that, in our judgment, assures our ability to provide an education that meets Mason standards."

Academics

The Krasnow Institute for Advanced Study is located on the Fairfax campus.

The university has strength in the basic and applied sciences with critical mass in proteomics, neuroscience and computational sciences. Research support comes to Mason faculty from such agencies as the National Institutes of Health, NASA, the National Science Foundation and the Defense Advanced Research Projects Agency. Likewise, the Center for Secure Information Systems is designated as a Center of Academic Excellence (CAE) as well as a Center of Academic Excellence in Research (CAE-R) in Information Assurance Education by the National Security Agency.

Mason's Center for History and New Media attracts more than one million visitors to its websites every month.

Mason's Center for Global Education's study abroad program has been rated highly offering dozens of programs ranging from one-week spring break programs to full year programs..

Mason's flagship Study Abroad experience is the prestigious Oxford Honors Program in which highly qualified students endure a rigorous application and interview process and, if selected, travel to the United Kingdom where they study for 6–12 months as matriculated students of Oxford University.

Mason was awarded $25 million in 2005 from the National Institute of Allergy and Infectious Diseases (NIAID), part of the National Institutes of Health, for construction of a Regional Biocontainment Laboratory at the Prince William Campus in Manassas.

Rankings

US News & World Report Undergraduate rankings include:

- 143rd (Tier 1) – National Universities Rankings 2011
- 1st – new category of "Up-and-coming National Universities" 2008
- 72nd – Top Public National Universities 2011
- 88th – Best Undergraduate Business Programs 2011
- 31st – The Systems Engineering and Operations Research Department for Best Engineering Schools in Industrial and Manufacturing, 2009

US News & World Report Graduate program rankings include:

- 42nd – Law 2010
- 51st – Political Science 2009
- 64th – History 2009
- 45th – Public Affairs 2008
- 63rd – Nursing 2007
- 65th – Education 2008
- 70th – Part time MBA 2011
- 8th – Industrial Organization Psychology PhD program 2001
- 63rd – Computer Science 2010

Other rankings:

- The School of Public Policy is ranked 1st in the nation for federally-funded public policy, public affairs, public administration and political science research.
- The university is ranked 58th in North America and 75th worldwide by the web-based Webometrics Ranking of World Universities
- 4th most diverse university in the nation, by the Princeton Review in 2008.
- 8th in the world political economy, 30th in public economics by econphd.net.
- As of 2008, the *Southern Economic Journal* ranks Mason economics as 3rd in Methodology and History of Economic Thought, 9th in General Economics and Teaching, 11th in Law and Economics, 25th in Public Economics and 25th in Microeconomics.

Schools and colleges

Research at Mason is organized into centers, laboratories, and collaborative programs. These include the College of Humanities and Social Sciences, the College of Education and Human Development, New Century College, the College of Health and Human Services, the College of Visual and Performing Arts, the Institute for Conflict Analysis and Resolution, the Krasnow Institute for Advanced Study, the School of Computational Sciences, the Volgenau School of Information Technology and Engineering, the School of Law, the School of Public Policy, the College of Science, and the School of Management. In addition, Mason's Office of the Provost includes research centers that deal with economics, global education, and teaching excellence.

In addition to a business undergraduate major and minor, Mason's School of Management has graduate programs for the Master of Business Administration degree (MBA) with a wide variety of concentrations/specializations, an Executive Master of Business Administration degree (EMBA), a Master of Science in Accounting (MSA), a joint MBA/MSA degree and a Master of Science in Technology Management degree.

Athletics

The school's sports teams are called the Patriots. The university's men's and women's sports teams participate in the NCAA's Division I, and are members of the Colonial Athletic Association, or CAA. The school's colors are green and gold. George Mason has two NCAA Division I National Championship to its credit; 1985 Women's Soccer and 1996 Men's Indoor Track & Field.

George Mason University was catapulted into the national spotlight in March 2006, when its men's basketball team advanced to the Final Four of the NCAA Men's Basketball Tournament by defeating the Michigan State Spartans, the defending champion North Carolina Tar Heels, the Wichita State Shockers, and the top-seeded Connecticut Huskies. Their "Cinderella" journey ended in the Final Four with a loss to the eventual tournament champion Florida Gators by a score of 73–58. As a result of the team's success in the tournament, the Patriots were ranked 8th in the final ESPN/USA Today Poll for the 2005–06 season. *The New York Times*,

The Washington Post, *Baltimore Sun*, and *USA Today* featured the story on their front pages, and was ranked by several publications as the sports story of the year.

The Patriots, who had never won an NCAA tournament game before 2006, became the first team from the CAA to crash the Final Four and were the first true mid-major conference team since 1979 to do so (that year, the Larry Bird-led Indiana State Sycamores as a #1 seed, and the Penn Quakers as a #9 seed both reached the Final Four). As #11-seeds, the 2006 Patriots also tied the 1986 LSU Tigers as the lowest-seeded team ever to reach the Final Four.

In 2008, the Patriots returned to the NCAA Tournament after winning the CAA Tournament. They were given a 12 seed and matched up against 5th-seeded Notre Dame. The Patriots were unable to make another miracle run, losing to the Irish by a score of 68–50.

Organizations

George Mason offers more than 200 clubs and organizations, including 16 fraternities, 15 sororities, 24 International-student organizations, 25 religious organizations, a student programming board, student government, club sports, debate team, and student media. The Office of Student Involvement at Mason administrates Student Government, Program Board, Fraternity and Sorority Life, Recognized Student Organization (RSO), Graduate and Professional Student Association (GAPSA), and Weekends at Mason (WAM). Mason also offers an Army ROTC program, called The "Patriot Battalion." Mason's club sports include ultimate frisbee, crew, equestrian, field hockey, football, lacrosse, underwater hockey, fencing, and rugby.

The George Mason University Forensics program is one of the top ranked competitive speech teams in the United States and has achieved international recognition in the field of communication studies. The team was founded in 1970 and has won nearly 10,000 individual speech awards. In 2010 the team placed 4th at the American Forensics Association National Tournament and won the International Forensics Association Championship. The Forensics Program has been extremely active on the George Mason campus with an active Community Service Committee. GMU hosts the annual Virginia is for Lovers collegiate speech tournament, the Patriot Games scholastic speech competition (which in 2009 had over 1,000 entries), and also will host the 2011 Catholic Forensics Association Grand National Tournament. Also, in 2010 Forensics students Brennan Morris, Colston Reid, Billy Strong, and Mickey Cox were George Mason University's highlight speakers at the State Legislature. Currently Dr. Peter Pober is the Program Director with Jeremy Hodgson as Assistant Director.

Media

Mason offers two regular print publications, *Broadside*, the student newspaper, and the *Mason Gazette*, the University-published newspaper. Mason also operates a Campus radio station, WGMU Radio. The online radio station offers music, entertainment, news, and public affairs relating to the University community, regional area and the country. The Mason Cable Network, or MCN, is the student organized and operated television station, and offers student produced entertainment and information on channel 89, available on the Fairfax campus of GMU. Mason also sponsors several student-run publications through its Office of Student Media, including the *VoxPop*, a feature magazine, Connect2Mason, an online media and news convergence Web site, *Volition*, an undergraduate student literary and art magazine, *Phoebe*, a graduate literary journal, *So to Speak*, a feminist literary journal, *GMView and Senior Speak*, an annual yearbook publication and video, *New Voices in Public Policy*, School of Public Policy student journal, and *Hispanic Culture Review*, a student bilingual (Spanish/English) journal on Hispanic literature and culture. Mason also sponsors several academic journals including, *TABLET, the International Affairs Journal of George Mason University*. Between approximately 1993 and 1998, the University was also the home of *The Fractal: Journal of Science Fiction and Fantasy*.

Between 1999 and 2005, the underground newspaper *Expulsion* was distributed on the Mason campus. It also experienced a brief online resurgence in 2007.

The staff of the Center for History and New Media produces a podcast called *Digital Campus*.

In fall 2008, the satirical online newspaper, *The Mason Squire*, premiered. The site featured fake news stories criticizing the university. The newspaper's mottos were "Because fake news doesn't report itself" and "Fake news just got a whole lot sexier". However, the site has been inactive since late 2009.

Fraternity and sorority life

George Mason University does not have traditional Fraternity & Sorority housing or a "Greek row." For several years, three Panhellenic Council organizations had established "Living/Learning Floors" in the University Commons. Alpha Omicron Pi had a floor 2004–2010, Gamma Phi Beta had a floor 2006–2010, and Alpha Phi had a floor 2007–2010.

Officially, Mason refers to "Greek Life" as "Fraternity & Sorority Life" to avoid confusion with the Hellenic Society club, a student organization focusing on the people and culture of Greece.

Most organizations in the Interfraternity Council (IFC) and Panhellenic Council (PHC) hold one or two large charitable events each year. Most organizations in the National Pan-Hellenic Conference (NPHC) and Multicultural Greek Council (MGC) hold a series of smaller charitable events throughout the year. The NPHC is also known for its annual Step Show.

The most well-known event associated with Fraternity & Sorority Life on campus is held each spring and is called Greek Week. This annual event includes competitive sporting and trivia events, charitable fund raising, and is usually ended with Greek Sing. Organizations participating in Greek Sing put together 10–15 minute themed shows which have included extravagant costumes, set designs, lighting displays, multimedia presentations, dances, singing, acrobatics, and more.

PHC holds a formal recruitment each fall. Informal recruitment is held in spring. Many PHC organizations also offer continuous open recruitment (or continuous open bidding) after the designated recruitment period. IFC has a designated one-week rush period in the fall and spring. This week is regulated and monitored, but participants are not registered or tracked.

Presidents past and present

- Lorin A. Thompson, (1966–73)
- Vergil H. Dykstra, (1973–1977)
- Robert C. Krug, (1977–1978)
- George W. Johnson, (1978–1996)
- Alan G. Merten, (1996–present)

Notable alumni

Corporate/non-profit

- Muna Abu-Sulayman, Secretary General and Executive Director, Alwaleed Bin Talal Foundation
- Zainab Salbi, President, Women for Women International
- Alan Harbitter, Chief Technology Officer, Nortel Government Solutions
- Raymond Winn, Partner, Deloitte & Touche
- Crystal R. Williams, Corporate Vice President of Contracts, VSE Corporation
- Roy Speckhardt, executive director of the American Humanist Association
- Yusuf Azizullah, consultant
- Will Seippel
- Martin Andrew Taylor, senior executive Corporate Vice President of Windows Live and MSN, and former Chief of Staff of the CEO of Microsoft Steve Ballmer
- Walter Anderson, American telephone enterpeneur

Government and politics

42nd Treasurer of the United States

Attorney General of Virginia

Deputy Chief of Staff to President George W. Bush

Commissioner of the U.S. Securities and Exchange Commission

- Anna E. Cabral, 42nd Treasurer of the United States under President George W. Bush
- William D. Hansen, United States Deputy Secretary of Education under President George W. Bush
- Liam O'Grady, United States federal judge
- Richard L. Young, United States federal judge
- Kathleen L. Casey, Commissioner of the U.S. Securities and Exchange Commission
- Juleanna Glover Weiss, Advisor to Vice President Dick Cheney
- John Morlu, Liberian Presidential Candidate
- Sean Connaughton, Virginia Secretary of Transportation, Former U.S. Maritime Administrator
- Ken Cuccinelli, Attorney General of Virginia (2010–)
- William W. Mercer, United States Attorney for the District of Montana
- Bob Deuell, Texas State Senator
- Deborah Hersman, Chairman, National Transportation Safety Board
- Mohammad Khazaee, Representative of the Islamic Republic of Iran to the United Nations
- Mark B. Madsen, Utah State Senator
- Mike Mazzei, Oklahoma State Senator
- Nancy Garland, member of the Ohio house of representatives
- David Bobzien, member of the Nevada Assembly
- Paul F. Nichols, Virginia House Delegate
- Kaye Kory, Virginia House Delegate
- James M. Scott, Virginia House Delegate
- Robert Traynham, Senior Republican Staffer, top aide to Senator Rick Santorum
- Nancy Pfotenhauer, adviser to the John McCain presidential campaign 2008
- Karl Rove, former Deputy Chief of Staff to President George W. Bush
- Steve Ricchetti, former Deputy Chief of Staff to President Bill Clinton
- William P. Winfree, NASA
- Michael Frey, member of the Fairfax

County Board of Supervisors
- Cathy Hudgins, member of the Fairfax County Board of Supervisors
- Sherri Kraham, deputy vice president at the Millennium Challenge Corporation
- Raynard Jackson, Republican political consultant
- Garrison Courtney, Chief Public Affairs of the Drug Enforcement Agency
- Denise Bode, energy expert, member of President George W. Bush Energy Transition Advisory Team

Literary and media
- Richard Bausch, novelist
- Robert Bausch, novelist
- Sharon Creech, novelist of children's fiction
- Carolyn Kreiter-Foronda, Poet Laureate of Virginia
- Mark Winegardner, author
- Rebecca Wee, poet
- Nancy K. Pearson, poet
- Nadine Meyer, poet
- Evan Oakley, poet
- J. Michael Martinez, poet
- Chad Ford, sports journalist and founder of ESPN Insider
- Clayton Swisher, Correspondent, Al Jazeera English
- Angie Goff, Traffic Presenter, WUSA-9 TV
- Hala Gorani, News Anchor, CNN
- Imad Musa, Senior Producer, The Riz Khan Show Al Jazeera English
- Stuart Cosgrove, Scottish journalist, broadcaster and television executive
- Brian Krebs, Journalist
- Stephen Moore, Journalist and Policy Analyst
- Susan Rook, former News Anchor, CNN & CNN Talkback Live
- Tom Knott, columnist at Washington Times

Sports and entertainment
- Julius Achon, Ugandan middle distance runner, currently holds the 800m American Collegiate Record
- Joe Addo, Soccer player
- Mark Adickes, Football player
- Negar Assari, Artist
- Kyle "K-Dog" Benham, Associate Producer/radio personality
- Abdi Bile, Olympic runner
- Lamar Butler, Basketball player and member of the 2006 NCAA Final Four team
- Shawn Camp, Baseball player, currently with the Toronto Blue Jays
- Folarin Campbell, Basketball player and member of the 2006 NCAA Final Four team
- Terri Dendy, Olympic track and field athlete
- Ben Dogra, sports agent
- Mark Pulisic, soccer player
- Charlie Raphael, soccer player
- Rebecca Cardon, actress
- John Driscoll, Actor
- Chad Dukes, radio host, WJFK-FM
- Jennifer Derevjanik, Basketball player
- Jerry Dunn, Basketball coach
- Mike Garrett, Soccer player
- Kristi Lauren Glakas, Miss Virginia Teen, Miss Virginia USA 2004, USA 1999 Miss Virginia 2005
- King Kamali, Iranian bodybuilder
- Archie Kao, Actor
- Mike Kohn, Olympic bobsledder
- Jai Lewis, Basketball player and member of the 2006 NCAA Final Four team
- Bob Lilley, Soccer player and head coach
- Tamir Linhart, Soccer player
- Jason Miskiri, Basketball player
- Dayton Moore, General Manager, Senior Vice President of Baseball Operations, Kansas City Royals
- Rob Muzzio, Decathlon Champion, Olympic Athlete
- Anthony Noreiga, Soccer player
- Gabe Norwood, Philippine Basketball Association player and member of the 2006 NCAA Final Four team
- John O'Hara, Soccer player
- Jennifer Pitts, Miss Virginia 2002, Miss Virginia USA 2005
- Maegan Phillips, Miss Virginia USA 2009
- Kenny Sanders, Basketball player
- George Evans, Basketball player
- Tony Skinn, Basketball player and member of the 2006 NCAA Final Four team
- Tommy Steenberg, Iceskater
- Will Thomas, Basketball player and member of the 2006 NCAA Final Four team
- Chris Widger, Baseball player
- Aimee Willard, Lacrosse player
- Ricky Wilson, Basketball player
- Carlos Yates, Basketball player
- Kate Ziegler, World record distance swimmer

Other
- Furqan Ahmed Nizami, Vice President: National Bank of Pakistan
- Steven Horwitz, Professor
- Edward Stringham, Professor
- Mark Perry (economist), Professor
- Jonathan Klick, Professor
- Jeb Livingood, Professor and writer
- M. Brian Blake, Professor
- Graham Foust, Professor and poet
- David Prychitko, Economist
- Deborah Willis, photographer and Professor
- Daniel Mann, lawyer
- Sandy Antunes, astronomer
- Anousheh Ansari, space tourist
- Amir Ansari
- Robert A. Levy, Chairman of the Cato Institute
- Mark A. Calabria, Director of Financial Regulation Studies at the Cato Institute
- Sibel Edmonds, former Federal Bureau of Investigation translator
- Jose Rodriguez, political activist
- Jon Gettman, marijuana reform activist and leader of the Coalition for Rescheduling Cannabis, longtime contributor to *High Times* magazine
- Joshua N. Weiss, Mediator
- Randall C. Berg, Jr.
- Victoria Stiles, makeup artist
- Kendrick Moxon
- Chris Harper
- Alolita Sharma, computer scientist
- Alan M. Davis
- Taylor Edgar, stand-up comic and musician
- Fred E. Foldvary, Economist
- Chris DiBona, Google Public Sector Director
- Michael L. Murray, American folklorist
- Matt Kibbe, President and CEO of FreedomWorks

- Stephen Slivinski, Senior economist for the Goldwater Institute
- Mark Kelner
- Angela Orebaugh, cyber security technologist and professor
- Eric Schansberg, economics professor
- George Michael, professor
- Brad Pfaff, U.S. Department of Agriculture's Wisconsin Farm Service Agency executive director

Notable faculty

College of Humanities and Social Sciences

- William Sims Bainbridge
- Shaul Bakhash, scholar of Persian studies. Husband of Haleh Esfandiari.
- Mary Catherine Bateson, daughter of American cultural anthropologist Margaret Mead, former Clarence J. Robinson Professor in Anthropology and English, now Professor Emerita.
- Robert Bausch, novelist
- Rei Berroa, poet
- Andrés Boiarsky
- Courtney Angela Brkic, poet
- Michael Bunn
- Arthur W. Chickering
- Alan Cheuse, novelist
- Wilfrid Desan
- Bùi Diễm, South Vietnam's Ambassador to the United States
- Robert J. Elder, Jr, Air Force Commander
- Marita Golden, novelist
- Gerald L. Gordon
- Joshua Greenberg
- Hugh Gusterson
- Helon Habila
- Deanna Hammond
- Frances V. Harbour
- Hugh Heclo, professor of American politics and winner of John Gaus award.
- Carma Hinton, documentary flimmaker. Credits include The Gate of Heavenly Peace
- Mark N. Katz
- Peter Klappert, poet
- Gary L Kreps
- Lawrence W. Levine, historian
- Suzannah Lessard, writer
- Samuel Robert Lichter, former professor at Princeton University, Georgetown University, George Washington University, Yale, and Columbia University.
- Peter Mandaville, professor of international affairs and scholar of political Islam.
- Nadine Meyer, poet
- Robert Nadeau, English professor
- Eric Pankey, poet
- Roy Rosenzweig
- Richard E. Rubenstein
- Martin Sherwin, Pulitzer Prize winner for his biography of Robert Oppenheimer
- Clare Shore
- Susan Shreve
- Richard Norton Smith Presidential historian & former director of five presidential libraries.
- Rod Smith, poet
- Peter Stearns, American historian and current provost
- Rex A. Wade, professor of Russian history.
- Roger Wilkins, Pulitzer Prize winner for coverage of the Watergate scandal (along with Bob Woodward and Carl Bernstein while he was working at The Washington Post.) Now retired.
- Margaret R. Yocom
- Mary Kay Zuravleff, novelist

Department of Economics

James M. Buchanan, Nobel Prize-winning economist

Vernon L. Smith, Nobel Prize-winning economist

Gordon Tullock, Developed the Public Choice theory

- Peter Boettke
- Kenneth E. Boulding, cofounder of the General Systems Theory
- Donald J. Boudreaux
- James M. Buchanan, Nobel Prize-winning economist (1986)
- Henry N. Butler
- Bryan Caplan
- Tyler Cowen
- Christopher Coyne
- Richard H. Fink, Executive Vice President of the Koch Industries
- Joseph L. Fisher, U.S. Congressman from Virginia
- Jack A. Goldstone
- Robin Hanson
- Laurence Iannaccone
- Manuel H. Johnson, Former Vice Governer of the Federal Reserve
- Arnold Kling
- Daniel B. Klein
- Don Lavoie
- Peter T. Leeson
- Kevin McCabe
- Maurice McTigue, former Minister for Labor in New Zealand
- Russell Roberts
- George Selgin
- Vernon L. Smith, Nobel Prize-

winning economist (2002)
- Alex Tabarrok
- Robert Tollison
- Gordon Tullock, Developed the Public Choice Theory
- Bruce Yandle, Executive Director of the Federal Trade Commission
- Richard E. Wagner
- Lawrence H. White
- Walter E. Williams, John M. Olin Distinguished Professor of Economics
- Bart Wilson

College of Science
- Abul Hussam, inventor of the Sono arsenic filter, for which he received the 2007 sustainability prize awarded by the National Academy of Engineering
- James Trefil, physicist, and author
- Edward Wegman, statistician
- Klaus Fischer (mathematician)
- David Albright
- Ernst Volgenau, chairman and founder of SRA International
- Jagdish Shukla, founding member of the International Centre for Theoretical Physics
- Robert Hazen, Clarence Robinson Professor of Earth Science, and author
- Caroline Crocker, American immunopharmacologist who teaches creationist claims about evolution
- Robert Axtell
- Boris Willis
- Peter J. Denning
- John P. Snyder, cartographer
- James Chesebro
- Yakir Aharonov, Israeli physicist
- Angela Orebaugh
- Suresh V. Shenoy
- Fred Singer
- Peter A. Freeman
- Ken Alibek, Colonel in the Soviet Union in charge of biodefense. He is an expert in biological warfare

School of Public Policy

United States Ambassador to Greece and Bosnia and Herzegovina

Michael Hayden, former director of the CIA

- Kenneth Button
- Desmond Dinan
- Michael Hayden, former CIA Director
- Zoltan Acs
- Louise Shelley
- Marc Gopin
- Seymour Martin Lipset
- Richard Florida
- John N. Warfield
- Patrick Michaels
- Stephen Haseler
- Bill Schneider (journalist), CNN's senior political analyst
- Thomas J. Miller, US Ambassador to Greece, and Bosnia and Herzegovina
- Patrick Mendis, US Diplomat
- Jeremy Shearmur
- Thomas M. Davis, former U.S. Congressman from Virginia
- William Conrad Gibbons
- Richard Norton Smith
- David S. Alberts, Director of Research for the Office of the Assistant Secretary of Defense

School of Management
- Jim Larranaga, Mason's head men's basketball coach since 1997, including the Final Four run
- Anthony Sanders, Distinguished Professor of Real Estate Finance
- Teresa J. Domzal, dean of the school of management
- Raymond W. Smith

School of Law
- Todd Zywicki, former Director of the Office of Policy Planning at the Federal Trade Commission
- Michael I. Krauss, former Commissioner for Québec's Human Rights Commission
- David Bernstein
- Henry Manne
- Clay T. Whitehead, former director of the White House Office of Telecommunications Policy
- Timothy Muris, former chairman of the Federal Trade Commission
- Deborah Platt Majoras, former chairman of the Federal Trade Commission
- William Kovacic, former member of the Federal Trade Commission
- William H. Lash, former United States Assistant Secretary of Commerce
- James LeMunyon, former United States Assistant Secretary of Commerce
- Jeremy A. Rabkin
- Henry N. Butler, Republican Candidate for member of the U.S. House of Representatives from Virginia's 11th congressional district
- Victoria Espinel, United States Intellectual Property Enforcement Coordinator
- Frank H. Buckley
- Raymond O'Brien
- Loren A. Smith, Federal Judge
- Susan Dudley, Administrator of the Office of Information and Regulatory Affairs under President George W. Bush
- Michael Uhlmann
- Sigrid Fry-Revere, founder and president of Center for Ethical Solutions
- Hans-Bernd Schäfer
- Peter Berkowitz

- Kyndra Miller Rotunda, Army JAG officer
- Leonard Liggio, Vice President of Atlas Economic Research Foundation
- Irving Kayton, founder of the Patent Resources Group, Inc. (PRG)
- William J. Roberts, copyright royalty judge
- Sandra Froman, President of the National Rifle Association of America
- Ernest Gellhorn
- James C. Miller III, Chairman of the Federal Trade Commission and Budget Director for President Ronald Reagan
- Chuck Robb, former Governor of Virginia and former U.S. Senator
- Douglas H. Ginsburg, judge on the United States Court of Appeals for the District of Columbia Circuit, and Ronald Reagan's nominee to the United States Supreme Court
- Lawrence J. Block, Federal Judge
- Adrian S. Fisher, lawyer, diplomat, and politician during the 60s and 70s

School of Recreation, Health, and Tourism
- Craig Esherick, former head coach of the Georgetown basketball team
- Charley Casserly, NFL General Manager of the Washington Redskins and Houston Texans
- Steve Baumann, Chief Executive of the National Soccer Hall of Fame

Accreditation
- Southern Association of Colleges and Schools

Source (edited): "http://en.wikipedia.org/wiki/George_Mason_University"

Ittihad University

Ittihad University (IU) is the first-largest private university located in the emirate of Ras Al Khaimah (RAK), United Arab Emirates.

Founded in year 1999 according to the Emiri Decree No. 9/99 issued by H.H. Sheikh Saqr Bin Muhammad Al-Qassimi, the Ruler of Ras Al Khaimah Emirate, Member of the Supreme Council.

The University also enjoys the support of H.H. Sheikh Saud Bin Saqr Al-Qassimi, the Crown Prince and Deputy Ruler of Ras Al Khaimah Emirate. The University was granted Official Candidacy to operate as an institution of higher education by COMMISSION FOR ACADEMIC ACCREDITATION, Ministry of Higher Education and Scientific Research United Arab Emirates.

The University is divided into four undergraduate colleges (schools) that encompass a broad range of academic fields and campuses boast large numbers of distinguished faculty.

Source (edited): "http://en.wikipedia.org/wiki/Ittihad_University"

RAKCODS

Ras Al-Khaimah College of Dental Sciences (**RAK CODS**) is a constituent college of the Ras al-Khaimah Medical and Health Sciences University (RAK MHSU) located in Ras al-Khaimah, United Arab Emirates. The university was established by the Ras Al Khaimah Human Development Foundation (RAK – HDF) under the leadership of His Highness Sheikh Saud bin Saqr al Qasimi, Crown Prince & Deputy Ruler of Ras Al Khaimah who is also Chancellor of the University. The RAK College of Dental Sciences offers a 5 Year Bachelor of Dental Surgery program, followed by a 1 year internship.

Mission and vision
Vision
To be a leading college of Dental Sciences in the Middle East dedicated to the pursuit of academic excellence by fostering, disseminating and applying knowledge and intellectual values to ensure an enriching future for the student community and preparing them to join the dental and oral health care field of the 21st Century.

Mission
RAK CODS is committed, through its BDS and upcoming Laser Dentistry programs in dental and oral health care, to prepare graduates who are able to develop critical skills in their practice and application of knowledge. The college is committed to equipping them with practical and clinical skills and knowledge and enabling them to make a valuable contribution to the communities in which they live and practice the art and science of Dentistry.

Degree program
The RAK CODS Bachelor of Dental Surgery (BDS) program is of five years duration followed by one year of internship.

The program comprises six months of general education, two years of basic medical and dental sciences and two-and-half years of clinical dental sciences. This is followed by a year of dental internship.

The curriculum has been developed to provide learning opportunities enabling dental students to acquire fundamental knowledge, develop basic skills and appropriate principles relevant to oral health care in the context of the community.

The graduates of this program shall have opportunities to work in general practice, the community dental service, hospital practice, university teaching and research in various individual organizations.

The BDS program has obtained Initial Accreditation from Ministry of Higher Education & Scientific Research, UAE and admission is in progress for the academic session commencing September 2009.

American University of Sharjah

Source (edited): "http://en.wikipedia. org/wiki/RAKCODS"

American University of Sharjah (**AUS**) (in Arabic: الجامعة الأمريكية في الشارقة) is an independent, not-for-profit coeducational higher educational institution in Sharjah, United Arab Emirates, founded in 1997 by Dr. Sultan bin Mohamed Al-Qasimi, Member of the UAE Supreme Council and Ruler of Sharjah. Its medium of instruction is English, and it is based on American-style universities. AUS consistently ranks among the top universities in the Middle East. The university is the flagship institution in Sharjah's 1,600-acre (6.5 km) University City, which incorporates a number of other universities, among which is the University of Sharjah.

History

On July 3, 2004, American University of Sharjah (AUS) was granted accreditation by the Middle States Commission on Higher Education in the United States of America. In its final report granting the university accreditation, the Middle States Commission on Higher Education, one of six regional U.S. accrediting agencies, congratulated AUS on its excellent roster of undergraduate and graduate programs, its state-of-the-art campus facilities, its highly qualified faculty and staff, and its dynamic student body. AUS was successful in completing the accreditation process in a relatively short period of time, a fact that was recognized and appreciated by the Commission in its report.

Main Building & Auditorium

The university became a candidate for accreditation in 2002 and subsequently embarked on an in-depth self-study as part of its application. An evaluation team from the Commission visited the university in March that year. The team, which included administrators and faculty from the United States, reviewed the self-study completed by the university, visited the campus and met with faculty, staff, students, administrators, alumni and employers of AUS graduates. Upon its return to the United States, the team submitted a report as well as its recommendation to the Commission for deliberation in its June meeting the campus and met with faculty, staff, students, administrators, alumni and employers of AUS graduates.

On September 17, 2006, all six of the bachelor of science programs in the College of Engineering at American University of Sharjah were granted accreditation by the Accreditation Board for Engineering and Technology (ABET), of the United States of America. With this prestigious international accreditation, AUS has become one of the first universities in the region and the second outside the United States to have its undergraduate programs receive ABET accreditation. The first being the American University in Cairo.

On June 28, 2010, AUS became a member of the Association of American Colleges and Universities (AAC&U) allowing the university to share its news, activities and accomplishments with the AAC&U community by taking part in their journals, leading workshops and attending its meetings. In addition. The School of Business and Management had entered the final stages of accreditation by the Association to Advance Collegiate Schools of Business (AACSB)

As of August 10, 2010, the College of Architecture, Art and Design has become a full member of the Association of Collegiate Schools of Architecture (ACSA), while its Bachelor of Architecture program became the first program outside of North America to be granted formal accreditation by the prestigious US-based National Architectural Accrediting Board (NAAB)

Campus

AUS sits on the southern edge of Sharjah and is approximately ten kilometers southeast of the center of the city and about fifteen kilometers from Dubai. The university offers a full range of amenities including a branch of Sharjah Islamic Bank, a health center, a pharmacy, a barbershop, a full gym, a sports complex, and full-facility dormitories.

Library

Completed in 2006, AUS Library is one of the biggest of its kind in the United Arab Emirates. Focusing on scholarly topics taught at AUS, the AUS Library offers a comprehensive collection to satisfy the needs of AUS students, and faculty. The university library houses a collection of more than 145,000 items, including 110,000 items (including books, CDs DVDs etc.), 50 000 electronic books, 262 journals in print, and 50 online databases and indexes that are accessible locally and remotely.

Unique to the university is the AUS Archives department, which is a repository for institutional records that created by various academic and administrative departments of the university. The mission of the Archives is to collect, maintain, preserve, and make available records that are of historical or legal value, as well as records that document the development of the university and the various campus activities.

Sharjah Training and Development Center

The Sharjah Training and Development Center (STDC) is a joint effort of the Sharjah Chamber of Commerce and Industry (SCCI) and the School of Business and Management at the American University of Sharjah (AUS) which aims to provide learning and development opportunities for businesses in Sharjah and the UAE. The two organizations signed a Memorandum of Understanding (MOU) to that effect on April 20, 2009.

The center aims to strengthen Sharjah as an international business hub and enhance the capabilities of local businesses and government organizations by providing life-long learning opportunities in courses and programs that integrate regional and global perspectives.

Undergraduate programs

College of Arts and Sciences

- Bachelor of Arts in English Language and Literature (BAELL)
o Concentration in English Language
o Concentration in English Literature
- Bachelor of Arts in International Studies (BAIS)
o Concentration in International Relations
o Concentration in International Economics
o Concentration in Western Studies
o Concentration in Arab Studies in a Global Context
- Bachelor of Arts in Mass Communication (BAMC)
o Concentration in Public Relations
o Concentration in Advertising
o Concentration in Journalism
- Bachelor of Science in Biology (BSB)
- Bachelor of Science in Chemistry (BSCH)
- Bachelor of Science in Environmental Science (BSES)
o Concentration in Environmental Biology and Ecosystems
o Concentration in Environmental Chemistry and Analysis
- Bachelor of Science in Mathematics (BSM)

College of Architecture, Art and Design

- Bachelor of Architecture (BArch)
- Bachelor of Interior Design (BID)
- Bachelor of Science in Design Management (BSDM)
- Bachelor of Science in Multimedia Design (BSMD)
- Bachelor of Science in Visual Communication (BSVC)

College of Engineering

- Bachelor of Science in Computer Science (BSCS)
- Bachelor of Science in Chemical Engineering (BSChE)
- Bachelor of Science in Civil Engineering (BSCE)
- Bachelor of Science in Computer Engineering (BSCoE)
- Bachelor of Science in Electrical Engineering (BSEE)
- Bachelor of Science in Mechanical Engineering (BSME)

School of Business and Management

- Bachelor of Arts in Economics (BAE)
- Bachelor of Science in Business Administration (BSBA)
o Concentration in Accounting
o Concentration in Finance
o Concentration in Management
o Concentration in Management Information Systems
o Concentration in Marketing

Graduate studies

Masters programs

- Master of Arts in Teaching English to Speakers of Other Languages (MATESOL)
- Master of Arts in English/Arabic/English Translation and Interpreting (MATI)
- Persian Gulf Executive Master of Public Administration (GEMPA)
- Master of Business Administration (MBA)
- Master of Science in Engineering Systems Management (MSESM)
- Master of Science in Mechatronics (MSMTR)
- Master of Science in Electrical Engineering (MSEE)
- Master of Science in Mechanical Engineering (MSME)
- Master of Science in Computer Engineering (MSCoE)
- Master of Science in Chemical Engineering (MSChE)
- Master of Science in Civil Engineering (MSCE)
- Master of Urban Planning (MUP)

Graduate certificates

- Graduate Certificate in Teaching English to Speakers of Other Languages (GCTESOL)
- Graduate Certificate in Urban Planning (GCUP)
- Graduate Certificate in Mechatronics Engineering (GCMTR)
- Graduate Certificate in Museum and Heritage Studies (GCMHS)

Student life

Green initiative

The university has always encouraged the awareness of having a green environment by offering related courses such as Sustainable Design for Architects and Environmental Engineering for Civil Engineers as well as regularly hosting seminars conducted by notable professors. The university has started to set itself as an example of green awareness by first and foremost creating the green SBM (School of Business and Management) building which began construction in Spring 2010 and scheduled to be fully operational by Fall 2011. The university has also taken a drastic step in Spring 2011 by banning smoking throughout the entire academic campus for students, faculty and staff alike except in the poorly ventilated small smokers room in the Student Center; obviously, this decision was rejected by many smokers but management is determined to keep it as they have introduced fines to force the members of their community to abide by the policy. These fines keep escalating for repetitive violators.

Student center

One of the main facilities is the student center complex that acts as the focal point for university students and houses many restaurants, a smokers room and other activities that aim to fulfil its community's needs. However, some students complain about the noisiness of loud music inside the food court that distract them while eating.

Student clubs

The primary role of the student clubs is

to promote dialogue, showcase student interests and hobbies, spread cultural diversity and partake in students' educational and personal growth by creating an engaging lifestyle inside and outside AUS. The clubs include several ethnic/national clubs and interest-oriented clubs, such as PowerHit Radio Club, that are registered with the Office of Student Affairs.

However, there are several clubs in the university that act independently and are not registered with OSA. Most of these clubs are clubs that are specific to the different departments and university programs that exist in the university, such as the INSA Student Association.

Student publications
The Leopard Newspaper

The Leopard is an official biweekly university newspaper that brings together the university's pursuits and achievement and puts them to pen. The Leopard bridges the gap between the administration and the student body, helping bring the university closer to the realization of a better institution. The Leopard prioritizes its duties to the students, covering their activities and accomplishments.

It is a creative platform for encouraging literary expression, and one of the many attempts of the university to broaden students' horizons in ways that are interesting to them. The publication has a reputation of allowing emerging artists from the university to display their artwork as well.

Criticism

The high standard of education being offered at AUS is a target of immense criticism by most of its students and alumni. Achieving a high grade point average is deemed impossible by a large percentage of the enrolled students. A GPA of 1.7 is granted on a percentage of 70%, which is the passing percentage and the A grade is on 95% and above. This makes scoring high immensely hard for students as the margin of scoring high with a good grade decreases tremendously. Additionally, it has come to notice that professors follow the 'forced grading system'. This means that a limited number of students will secure the top grades (A or B), whereas a majority will lie in the middle i.e. the C range. Students who have either transferred to similar American universities in Cairo, Beirut or Dubai have been known to score higher, with the same amount of effort they put in at AUS. Some argue that the 'forced grading system' induces a more competitive environment differentiating AUS students from other University Graduates in the region. However, when it comes to transfers to other universities or graduate admissions, most AUS students do face difficulties in securing admissions and scholarships, regardless of the fact that AUS reaps its reputation as an institution that provides a highly competitive environment. The competitive environment notion is simply ignored by other universities in this regard as AUS refuses to provide percentages along with the GPA scales on its official transcripts.

Due to the Global Financial Crisis, AUS declared a reduction of its non-academic work staff by 5% due to the "uncertain conditions" of the economy. AUS Chancellor Peter Heath further indicated that tuition would increase by 12% for the academic year 2009/2010, bringing tuition up to Dh73,000 per year . In response to the changes, disgruntled AUS students launched a facebook group (NO! For the American University of Sharjah Annual Fees Raise) and a petition that would be sent to AUS President Sheikh Sultan bin Mohamed Al-Qasimi. Nevertheless, no solution was found on the issue and the tuition increase went ahead.

Furthermore, AUS announced the imposition of a rule that required students to pay an annual Dh2,500 fee that would be used to purchase books or stationery at the university bookstore. Any unused balance from the Dh2,500 will be forwarded for one academic year only. After that, the unused balance will expire and automatically transferred to a scholarship fund. The university stated that the new rule was created in order to abide by international copyright laws. However, this development caused a controversy that gained nationwide media attention in the UAE through news outlets such as Gulf News and The National.

As a result, AUS students launched a stronger petition in order to stop the new rule from passing. Chancellor Heath responded, "Faculty and, less frequently, students have complained for a number of years about the breaches in academic integrity and international copyright rules that result from significant copying of course materials by students. If we as a university do not seek to enforce these rules, then who will?". Eventually, the petition as well as internal university negotiations decreased the annual fee to Dh1,800. However, the issue of leftover money being automatically transferred to a scholarship fund still exists.

Notable alumni

- Sheikha Lubna Khalid Al Qasimi, Minister for Foreign Trade and former Minister of Economic and Planning (2004–2008); first woman to hold a ministerial post in the UAE
- Mahmood Abdul Ghaffar, Lead singer of Bahrain-based heavy metal/thrash metal band Motör Militia
- Mishal Hamed Kanoo, Deputy Chairman of Kanoo Group
- Sheikh Rashid bin Humaid Al Nuaimi, Chairman of Ajman Municipality and Planning and Chief of Ajman Club; son of Sheikh Humaid bin Rashid Al Nuaimi, ruler and emir of Ajman
- Hamad AlHamad, Administrator, Settlement & Central depository of financial securitites, Bahrain.

Notable professors

- Jack Swanstrom, professor of film; award-winning film maker
- James Onley, historian and expert on Persian Gulf studies
- Mohammed Ibahrine, assistant professor of mass communication and advertising
- Said Faiq, professor of translation, interpreting and intercultural studies
- Samih Farsoun, professor emeritus of sociology; founding dean of the College of Arts and Sciences in AUS

Gallery

View of the main building of AUS

View of the main building of AUS

View of the library

View of the engineering departments

University City seen from AUS
Source (edited): "http://en.wikipedia.org/wiki/American_University_of_Sharjah"

ECUoS

The College of Engineering at The University of Sharjah was established in 1997 by a decree from His Highness Sheikh Dr. Sultan bin Mohamed Al-Qasimi, member of the UAE Supreme Council, Ruler of Sharjah, and the Supreme President of the University. The vision of His Highness for The University of Sharjah was to be a beacon of knowledge that serves the society by providing quality higher education to its youth and playing a major role in the technological development of the UAE. In practical terms, this meant that a new university with a significant College of Engineering was established in the Middle-East that had significant funding and that was owned and directed by the ruler of a state. This allowed many students of the region to study and graduate while remaining in an environment that is more culturally appropriated than Western universities such as those of the USA, UK or Australia. This is especially valid for female Muslim students. In fact, 2/3 of the students of the University of Sharjah were female in the years 2006-2010. In the College of Engineering, there was also a higher proportion of female students which is a phenomenon that is opposite to what is observed in most western countries such as Australia where there are special programs aimed at boosting the number of female students studying engineering.

In the College of Engineering at the University of Sharjah, more than 1000 students were enrolled in 2010; these were distributed among five undergraduate degree programs in Architectural, Civil, Computer, Electrical & Electronics and Industrial Engineering and Management. Year 2004 marked the launch of three accreditation-eligible Masters Degree programs in Civil, Computer, and Electrical & Electronics Engineering, as well as a new focus in research.

The College management structure, processes andmmission were dramatically revised during the Deanship of Prof Boashash so as to focus on effectiveness, maintaining a position at the forefront of knowledge to graduate talented and qualified engineers who are capable of playing an active role in the continuing development of their chosen profession, supporting the needs of the local industry and society, and contributing to the culture of Sharjah. The College placed strong emphasis on innovative teaching and learning methodologies and developed state of the art curricula emphasizing analysis, design and hands-on experience for all students, with engineering concepts being taught up-front. The adopted teaching philosophy was based on collaborative teaching with emphasis on lifelong learning, self-learning, effective communication and teamwork. The development and improvement of programs were based on the same philosophy and methodology that the Dean, Prof Boashah implemented previously in Australia. The College of Engineering has excellent, state-of-the-art lecture halls and laboratories, but had a serious challenge in building genuine research facilities to meet the national and regional needs as well as becoming a genuine internationally-recognized research institution.

The College was committed to a close relationship between faculty, students and industry professionals through joint meetings, projects, workshops and conferences such as the top International Symposium on Signal Processing and its Applications (ISSPA 2007), ICM 2008 and WoSPA 2008 as well as several others that were introduced under the leadership of Prof Boashash as part of a strategic plan that was developed to show and monitor progress with actual milestones and outcomes; a brief summary is given below.

VISION

The College of Engineering at the University of Sharjah will be, and will be recognized as, an influential purposeful contributor to the technological development & welfare of the community.

MISSION

The College of Engineering at the University of Sharjah aims to contribute to the empowerment and advancement of the community, and to inspire and nurture a generation of responsible citizens through: 1) providing purposeful and quality engineering education; 2) conducting relevant research and promoting principled scholarship; 3) providing quality dedicated Community service; and 4) providing an effective admin. & mgmt. system

OBJECTIVES

The general aims of the College of Engineering are as follows: To provide a high quality, intellectually challenging education that prepares our graduates to make a positive contribution to society. To provide sufficient breadth and depth of knowledge to satisfy the accreditation requirements of the professional institutions. To equip students to learn for themselves both at university and throughout life, through mastery of a wide range of transferable skills. To provide training in research, leading to higher degrees within a stimulating and supportive environment. To make a significant contribution to the knowledge and understanding of engineering at national and international levels. To act as a focus and source of engineering expertise for local industry, including provision of Continuing Professional Development training

Departments

- Civil and Environmental Engineering Department
- Electrical and Computer Engineering Department
- Architectural Engineering Department
- Industrial Engineering and Management Department

Source (edited): "http://en.wikipedia.org/wiki/ECUoS"

Etisalat University College

Etisalat University College is a private university for men that was established by Etisalat for engineering and is located in the Sharjah, United Arab Emirates, with programs in Engineering and Applied Sciences. It has a department for Communication engineering, Computer engineering, Electronic engineering, and General Studies. The college has been merged with Khalifa University of Science, Technology and Research (KUSTAR).

Source (edited): "http://en.wikipedia.org/wiki/Etisalat_University_College"

Skyline University College (Sharjah)

Skyline University College Sharjah is owned by Kamal Puri (who is a Sindhi person) and is an Indian administered private educational institute located in Sharjah, United Arab Emirates. It is located in University City of Sharjah.

Skyline University College (known as Skyline College until 2008) was established in 1990 with the aim of responding innovatively and effectively to the training and educational needs of industries like aviation, hospitality, travel and tourism, computers, marketing, business management and finance sectors.

Skyline University conducts a four-year degree program, Bachelor in Business Administration majors in Travel & Tourism Management, Information Systems, International Business and Marketing.

Skyline University College has been operational since 1990. Its programs are supported with regular evaluation and academic boards, IT integration, 98% Ph.D. faculties, exclusive timings, high employment rate, scholarship, student feedback, etc. The campus in University city of Sharjah, situated on the border of Sharjah and Dubai, features modern academic and administrative blocks, Sports Center and a library.

The high level of doctorate holders is questionable. Lecturers join the college without holding a doctorate degree and two years later hold a doctorate degree.

The programs offered to the students by Skyline University College were fully approved and accredited by Ministry of Higher Education and Scientific Research, UAE from Autumn 2006 onwards. Skyline University College has articulation agreements with various colleges/universities in Australia, Canada, New Zealand, United Kingdom, USA, etc., which facilitates the students to be transferred to these colleges for further studies. Skyline University College also maintains professional relationships with IATA-UFTAA and IATA-FIATA.

Undergraduate programs

Skyline University College offers Bachelor's Degrees in:
- Business Administration with a majors in:
  - Travel & Tourism Management,
  - Information Systems,
  - International Business, and
  - Marketing.

Postgraduate programs

Skyline University College offers Master's Degrees, with an emphasis on:
- Marketing
- Finance

Accreditation

The Commission for Academic Accreditation (CAA) of the Ministry of Higher Education and Scientific Research, UAE. has approved Skyline University College Sharjah and accredited its programs..

Source (edited): "http://en.wikipedia. org/wiki/Skyline_University_College _(Sharjah)"

University City of Sharjah

Sharjah University City is an educational district of higher learning in the city of Sharjah, United Arab Emirates located close to the Sharjah International Airport. It contains the American University of Sharjah, the Higher Colleges of Technology (Sharjah Men's College and Sharjah Women's College) and the University of Sharjah. The area also includes the Sharjah Police Academy, Sharjah Teaching Hospital and the Sharjah Library.

Source (edited): "http://en.wikipedia.org/wiki/University_City_of_Sharjah"

University of Sharjah

The **University of Sharjah** is a semi-governmental higher educational institution. Its founder, Supreme President and Chairman is the Ruler of Sharjah Sheikh Dr. Sultan bin Mohamed Al-Qasimi himself. Founded 1997, the University of Sharjah aims to meet the Emirate of Sharjah's educational and cultural needs within its Islamic values and tradition. Its vision is to become a leading academic institution in the Middle East and be well recognized around the world. The university is divided into two campuses — a men's campus and a women's campus.

Location

The main campus for the University of Sharjah is located on the southern edge of Sharjah in Sharjah University City near the Sharjah International Airport and is fifteen kilometres away from the center of the city. The community college provides its services through five branches located in different geographic areas in the Emirate of Sharjah such as Khor Fakkan, Kalba, and Dibba Al-Hisn.

Mission statement

The University of Sharjah aims to fulfill its obligations and responsibilities towards its students; add to human knowledge and scientific research; meet the needs of society; and enhance higher education in the country in coordination with other institutions of higher learning.

Academics

The university is compromised by the following colleges and their departments:

- College of Sharia'a & Islamic Studies
- Foundation of Religion
- Jurisprudence and its Foundations
- College of Arts, Humanities and Social Sciences
- Arabic Language and Literature
- English Language and Literature
- History and Islamic Civilization
- Sociology, Department of Education
- English Language Center
- College of Sciences
- Computer Science
- Chemistry, Mathematics
- Applied Physics
- Applied Biology
- College of Business Administration
- College of Engineering
- Architectural Engineering
- Civil and Environmental Engineering
- Electrical and Computer Engineering
- Industrial Engineering and Management
- College of Health Sciences
- MEDICAL LABORATORY TECHNOLOGY
- MEDICAL DIAGNOSTIC IMAGING
- NURSING
- PHYSIOTHERAPY
- HEALTH SERVICES ADMINISTRATION
- ENVIRONMENTAL HEALTH
- CLINICAL NUTRITION AND DIETETICS
- College of Law
- College of Fine Arts & Design
- Fashion Design and Textile
- Fine Arts
- Graphic Design and Multimedia
- Interior Architecture
- Jewelery Design
- College of Communication
- Mass Communication
- Public relations
- College of Medicine
- Basic Medical Science
- Clinical Science
- Family Community Medicine & Behavioral Sciences
- College of Dentistry
- General and Specialist Dental Practice
- Oral & Craniofacial Health Sciences
- College of Pharmacy
- Clinical Pharmacy
- Pharmacology and Pharmaceutics
- The Community College
- College of Graduate Studies & Research

Source (edited): "http://en.wikipedia.org/wiki/University_of_Sharjah"

ALHOSN University

ALHOSN University is an educational institution founded in 2005 located in Abu Dhabi, the capital city of the United Arab Emirates. ALHOSN University has three faculties containing a total of nine departments.

History

Founded in 2005 by Abu Dhabi Holding Company in response to growing local demand for high-quality educational institutions, the university was named after the historic ALHOSN Palace in the emirate of Abu Dhabi. The ALHOSN board ordered the development of a world-class curriculum through the assistance of experienced North American educators and the adoption of services based on best educational sector practices. The university opened its doors to an initial batch of 94 students under five undergraduate programs.

ALHOSN Palace

Sheikh Shakhboot Bin Zayed Al Nahyan built it as a castle when the seat of government was moved from the Liwa Oasis to the Abu Dhabi Island in 1793.

Academic information

ALHOSN presently offers 11 undergraduate and 7 graduate programs accredited by the UAE Ministry of Higher Education and Scientific Research (Commission for Academic Accreditation) and oversees an English Language Center and a Continuing Education Center. It publishes the *ALHOSN University Journal of Engineering and Applied Sciences*, a biannual refereed journal.

Faculties

- Faculty of Engineering & Applied Sciences
- Faculty of Business
- Faculty of Arts & Social Sciences

Campuses and buildings

The university's City Campus includes the Men's Campus, the Women's Campus, a Library Building, a Lectures Building, an Engineering Labs Building and a Studio Building. A world-class main campus is being planned. Students of all nationalities and those with special needs are accepted, and women are encouraged to join the engineering programs.

Admissions

An estimated 1,400 students during the spring of 2009 and an 831% increase in the 2009 summer enrolment over the past three years. Several service and facility upgrades where implemented in 2009, including the construction of a new Studio Building.

Web-based services

- Official website
- Online students portal
- Web-based course management system.
- Library system

The University uses the Moodle system for e-learning.

Source (edited): "http://en.wikipedia.org/wiki/ALHOSN_University"

Abu Dhabi University

Abu Dhabi University (ADU) was established in 2003, after three years of planning by H. H. Sheikh Hamdan Bin Zayed Al Nayhan and other distinguished citizens of the United Arab Emirates.

The University has stated:
The founders of the University envisioned an institution that would be among the best in the UAE, the Persian Gulf region and throughout the world.
—

Accreditation

The university aimed to ensure that all degree programs would be accredited by the Ministry of Higher Education and Scientific Research before any students enrolled.

Colleges and programs

Abu Dhabi University provides both undergraduate and postgraduate study programs, and consists of three collages along with the

- English Language Institute (ELI)
- the College of Arts & Sciences (CAS)
- the College of Business Administration (COBA)
- the College of Engineering and Computer Science (CECS).

Abu Dhabi University has affiliations with the following institutions: ENPC MBA Paris, Al Maktoum Institute, Universitat Klinikumbonn, University of Westminster, University of London, Thunderbird, University of Bath, Technische Universitat Munchen, Penn State SMEAL College of Business, HEC Paris, Freie Universitat Berlin, Monash University, National University of Singapore, Wollongong, Cranfield University, University of Victoria, Pearson, Edexcel International.

Abu Dhabi Campus

In October 2006, a new campus opened in Khalifa City, Abu Dhabi. It will include a teaching hospital, a mosque, a graduate center and a sports field. There are plans to build a K-12 school with a nursery that will cater to 2,000 students. The construction plan was divided into three phases. First Phase included an area of 43,000 square meters, a total of 50 classrooms, 6 computer labs, 2 scientific labs, 8 specialized labs and an auditorium with a seating capacity of 630, along with other various facilities. Phases two and three included expansion of facilities, increasing total capacity to 10,000 students.

Location

The University's Abu Dhabi campus is located on Al Ain Road, approximately 28 kilometers (km) from the city. The Al-Ain campus is located on the Abu Dhabi–Al Ain Road, near the Asharej Roundabout.

Source (edited): "http://en.wikipedia.org/wiki/Abu_Dhabi_University"

Al Ain University of Science and Technology

Al Ain University of Science and Technology (AINU, in Arabic: جامعة العين للعلوم و التكنولوجيا) was established in 2005 and is located in the city of Al Ain, within the Emirate of Abu Dhabi, United Arab Emirates.

Overview

An initiative of Sheikh Zayed Bin Sultan Al Nahyan, the late President of the UAE, the intention behind establishing Al Ain University of Science and Technology was to nurture and develop UAE residents to better contribute to the development of the UAE as well as respond to the challenges of the 21st century technology and mass media. In 2007, Al Ain University opened a branch in Abu Dhabi. The university aims to meet the needs of the job market in engineering, information technology, health professions, and business administration.

AINU Offers Bachelor degrees in:
- Accounting
- Finance and Banking
- Management Information Systems
- Teacher education
- Software Engineering
- Computer Science
- Computer Engineering
- Network and Communication Engineering
- Pharmacy
- Law

Accreditation

AINU is a licensed CAA institution by the UAE Ministry of Higher Education and Scientific Research, with 11 accredited degrees.

Total students

There were 1,100 students as of September 2007.

Gender ratio

The student popular is 60% male.

Admission

There are intakes in February and August. Applications accepted in final week before class starts.

Financial aid

Discounts are available for siblings or for academic excellence. Up to 50% discount for spouses and children of faculty members. The University provides loans to students experiencing financial hardship.

Source (edited): "http://en.wikipedia.org/wiki/Al_Ain_University_of_Science_and_Technology"

Masdar Institute of Science and Technology

The **Masdar Institute of Science and Technology** (Masdar Institute) is a graduate level, research-oriented university which is focused on alternative energy, sustainability, and the environment. It is located in Masdar City in Abu Dhabi, United Arab Emirates.

Masdar Institute is an integral part of the non-profit side of the Masdar Initiative and will be the first institution to occupy Masdar City. The Technology and Development Program at the Massachusetts Institute of Technology is providing scholarly assessment and advice to Masdar Institute.

History

Masdar Institute was established on February 25, 2007 and has commenced with 170 students from 32 countries in spring 2011. The establishment of Masdar Institute is part of a resource diversification policy for the Emirate of Abu Dhabi. Abu Dhabi's leadership views research and education in alternative energy as a keystone for the future development of the emirate and have expressed their commitment through the establishment of Masdar Initiative, Masdar City and the Zayed Future Energy Prize.

The President, Fred Moavenzadeh, was appointed in June 2010 and is the James Mason Crafts Professor of Systems Engineering and Civil and Environmental Engineering at MIT.

Campus

The campus, like Masdar City, is designed by architectural firm Foster + Partners and the first phase of the project is managed by CH2M HILL. Emphasis is placed on flexibility, use of traditional architectural elements and modern materials to provide for an optimized combination of natural lighting and cooling that minimize energy needs both indoors and outdoors.

Organization

Masdar Institute is emphasizing interdisciplinary collaboration and an early decision was made to establish programs rather than departments. The currently existing programs are:
- Chemical Engineering
- Mechanical Engineering
- Material Science and Engineering
- Engineering Systems and Management
- Water and Environmental Engineering
- Computing & Information Science
- Electrical Power Engineering
- Microsystems

Students

Masdar Institute has admitted 92 students from 22 countries in the first year of its operation and is planning to have a steady state population of about 800 students. Qualified students from around the world are offered a full tuition scholarship, monthly stipend, travel reimbursement, personal laptop, textbooks, and accommodation once accepted to any of Masdar Institute's programs.

Faculty and Research

Masdar Institute commenced teaching

in September 2009. They will be conducting research individually and in collaboration with MIT on a variety of topics.

Source (edited): "http://en.wikipedia.org/wiki/Masdar_Institute_of_Science_and_Technology"

Paris-Sorbonne University Abu Dhabi

Paris-Sorbonne University Abu Dhabi (PSUAD) or **Université Paris-Sorbonne Abu Dhabi (UPSAD)** is a French speaking university in Abu Dhabi, the capital city of the United Arab Emirates.

An international agreement between the French University Paris-Sorbonne or Paris IV, one of the most prestigious universities throughout the world, and the government of Abu Dhabi has been signed on 19 February 2006 to bring in Abu Dhabi the best international standards in higher education. Then PSUAD was established on 30, May 2006 by a decree of the ruler of the Emirate of Abu Dhabi (United Arab Emirates). The establishment of the university demonstrates the keenness of Abu Dhabi to create an international hub in culture and education as the establishment of the Louvre Abu Dhabi museum in 2007 shows as well.

The University opened its doors on 7 October 2006 in a temporary building. On 6 December 2009, PSUAD moved into its permanent campus on Reem island. PSUAD campus features approximately 93,000m2 of newly built, teaching and recreational facilities, including accommodation for students, a library that accommodates 200,000 books, a 700-seated guest-auditorium, a sports centre and a spacious cafeteria. It is worth mentioning that the DH 1.6bn campus comes to translate the shared vision of the government of Abu Dhabi and the government of France.

PSUAD remains true to the same teaching structure implemented in Paris. The campus of Abu Dhabi offers a whole array of subjects as in Sorbonne-Paris and Paris-Descartes. Its teachings are exclusively delivered by lecturers from the Paris following the European Credit Transfer System (ECTS). PSUAD is a full part of the European higher education area (or Bologna process), the European unified system of higher education. The teaching language is French. Paris Descartes University or Paris V is a partner for the Economics, Law and Political Sciences programmes. The degrees are French degrees.

(European Licence = 3-year undergraduate programmes)
- Economics and Management
- French and Comparative Literature
- Geography & Urban Planning
- History – Civilizations and International Affairs
- Archaeology and History of Art
- International Business and Languages
- Law and Political Science
- Philosophy and Sociology
- Information and Communication (3rd year specialisation, and in Paris only).

Master Programmes
- International Law, Diplomacy and International Relations
- Teaching French as a foreign language
- Marketing, Management, Communication and Media
- Urban & Regional Planning
- Business and Languages
- History of Art and Museum Studies
- Sustainable Development *(Upcoming Programmes)*
- Arts and Performance Management *(Upcoming Programmes)*

PSUAD is a common place to meet a student who had no prior mastery of French language ultimately speaking French fluently and self-assuredly in a year's time. The Intensive French Course prepares students' integration into the Licence Programmes.

PSUAD is ruled by Abu Dhabi Education Council (ADEC). PSUAD is managed by a board of six members, three of whom are appointed by Paris-Sorbonne University, the other three are appointed by Abu Dhabi Executive Council. PSUAD President is Paris-Sorbonne President and chairman of the board according to the agreement.

The research programmes at PSUAD benefit from the world class research work carried out in the field of humanities and social sciences at Université Paris-Sorbonne and Paris-Descartes. Upon completion of their undergraduate studies in Abu Dhabi, students will be able to choose whether to carry on with one of the Master programmes in Abu Dhabi or to join one of the departments in Paris where some of the world's most renowned professors will guide them through their research, covering fields as varied as medieval Islam, intercultural processes, travel literature, national and international geopolitics and will allow each student to find support wherever their field of interest is.

Highlighting the importance of dialogue between cultures, and the exchange of knowledge, PSUAD organises all year round lectures, round table discussions and colloquia hosting renowned experts from the region and beyond to shed the light on key aspects and phenomena in a wide range of fields. Most of these functions are open to public and provide simultaneous translation into Arabic and English.

The university residence offers one type of rooms; that is the single accommodation. Two residence blocks are available; one for male students and another for female students. The university residence is adjacent to the main campus to facilitate students' daily commute. PSUAD campus is located near the center of Abu Dhabi city which makes it close to main landmarks and attractions.

Sorbonne-Abu Dhabi lecturer Nasser Ben Ghaith was arrested for making pro-democracy remarks in April 2011, alonside two other pro-democracy campaigners including blogger Ahmed Mansoor.

Petroleum Institute

The **Petroleum Institute (PI)** is a private engineering school in Sas Al Nakhl, Abu Dhabi, United Arab Emirates, focused primarily on petroleum engineering and research, and funded by several major international oil companies. The goal of the institute is to provide the local oil and gas industry with highly skilled engineers.

The Institute was established in 2000 by an Emiri decree under the direction of His Highness Sheikh Khalifa bin Zayed Al Nahyan, ruler of Abu Dhabi and the president of the United Arab Emirates. It is financed and governed by a consortium of five major oil companies: ADNOC, Royal Dutch Shell, BP, Total S.A., and Japan Oil Development Company, a wholly owned subsidiary of INPEX.

The PI admitted its first students in the Fall of 2001. At present, over 800 undergraduate male students and 100 female students are studying in one of the following five engineering disciplines: Mechanical Engineering, Petroleum Engineering, Electrical Engineering, Chemical Engineering, and Petroleum Geosciences Engineering. As of Fall 2010, two new departments have been added: polymer science and material science. The Petroleum Institute also offers graduate level programs.

Source (edited): "http://en.wikipedia.org/wiki/Petroleum_Institute"

Source (edited): "http://en.wikipedia.org/wiki/Paris-Sorbonne_University_Abu_Dhabi"

Shaikh Khalifa Bin Zayed Bangladesh Islamia School

Shaikh Khalifa Bin Zayed Bangladesh Islamia School & College is a prominent educational institute providing sound academic education to Bangladeshi and international students in Abu Dhabi, UAE, for secondary and higher secondary education. It is a place where students are encouraged to increase their personal and social skills for the development of positive and effective young citizens in harmony with the global community. The School uses a wide range of educational books and materials to meet the needs of quality education for different cultures. Special emphasis is given to English, Arabic, Bengali, and Islamic Studies for Muslim students in Abu Dhabi, United Arab Emirates.

Location and climate
S.K.B.Z.Bangladesh Islamia School and College is located at **Muroor, Abu Dhabi**, United Arab Emirates, about 15 km south of Abu Dhabi, the capital of United Arab Emirates.

History

School front view.

Shaikh Khalifa Bin Zayed Bangladesh Islamia School, Abu Dhabi was founded on 23 August 1980 with the objective of imparting quality education to Bangladeshi community children. The infant institution of the 1980 has under gone a lot of uncertainties, hurdles and odds uncounted. Nevertheless, the only centre for the education of our community has finally been able to erect its head like that of a big banyan tree in a foreign land, far from Bangladesh, our dearest homeland.The selfless social workers of the community with the active co-operation of Bangladesh Embassy, Abu Dhabi managed to get the permission of Ministry of education and started holding classes in the afternoon with a handful of students from class I to V at Al Rashidiya Government School at Madina Zayed which later on shifted to Al Karama Street. The school kept running over there until 1990. His Highness Shaikh Zayed Bin Sultan Al Nahyan noble founder & father of U.A.E, donated a land of 80,000 sq ft (7,400 m). The present President of U.A.E. His Highness Shaikh Khalifa Bin Zayed Al Nahyan donated money for the construction of school building.

In 1990, Shaikh Khalifa Bin Zayed Bangladesh Islamia School came into being as a full fledged educational institution and started functioning in its own building in the heart of the capital city of Abu Dhabi. The school has English and Bengali medium from KG to 12th class. Since its inception, school has been following Dhaka Board's curriculum in Bengali & English Medium. School was affiliated in 1988 and the college section was opened in 1991. Salaries of the teachers & staff are met up from the tuition fees only. The boys and girls are separated from class VI to class XII level. This school building was not sufficient to accommodate all the students in one shift. Two separate shifts for the boys and girls were going on for a long time. It was essential to make a new academic building for the boys. But due to shortage of fund it has been not possible. In the year 2004 the Bangladesh Embassy and the present Executive committee took a noble initiative to construct a new academic building. With the help of handsome donation of Bangladeshi community and some other foreigners it has finally been possible to construct a new academic building at the cost of 1.2 million Dirham.

English is now the only means of popular communication. Due to this global demand of English language ma-

48 - Shaikh Khalifa Bin Zayed Bangladesh Islamia School

jority non-resident Bangladeshi of Abu Dhabi are sending their wards to the other foreign schools for study in English Medium only.The construction of the Boys' wing for bringing the school in one shift is another landmark in the history of school. This formidable task has been possible due to positive response of our kind Community members and their gracious donation. For all these things, we owe a lot to all concerned. We can all be up and doing for what is left to be done. We owe a lot to all the donors who supported the ongoing development of the school either by cash or kind.

Administration
The H. E. Ambassador of Bangladesh Embassy is the chief patron of the school. The School is run by a number of Executive Committee members who make the decisions to control the overall school affairs. The Principal and Vice Principal are responsible for academic affairs and solving various academic related issues. The first Executive Committee was established in 1980. It changes every year.

Academic structure
The present curriculum is under the board of Secondary and Higher Secondary Education, Dhaka, Bangladesh. The final examination of SSC and HSC are evaluated in GPA grading policy. The classes are conducted from KG to Grade 12 in English and Bengali Medium. There is a possibility to conduct 'O' level and 'A' level in the near future.

Facilities

Computer Laboratory.

Physics Laboratory.

Chemistry Laboratory.

Auditorium

Mosque

- **Computer Lab**
30 brand computers and a very convenient room to provide international standard computer Education is available here. 24 hours Internet facility in our computer laboratory.
- **Physics Lab**
The physics lab has the modern equipment to meet the highest standard.
- **Biology Lab**
The biology lab has numerous practical equipments for the enrichment of biological studies.
- **Chemistry Lab**
This lab has the up-to-date technologies to meet the standards of the chemistry studies.
- **Library**
The library consists of around 10,000 books.
- **Transport**
It has fully air-conditioned buses and the network covers most of the city of Abu Dhabi, Shahama, Musaffah, Baniyas, Mafraq, Rahaba, Al-Wathba, Khalifa City.
- **Recreation**
There is a big field and auditorium for both indoor and outdoor games. It is also used for different cultural activities like an annual cultural program, Debate Competition, etc.
- **Mosque**
These is a mosque for religious practice and prayer.
- **Scholarships**
Scholarships are awarded for meritorious students. Free studentships are awarded to the same siblings and needy families.
Source (edited): "http://en.wikipedia.org/wiki/Shaikh_Khalifa_Bin_Zayed_Bangladesh_Islamia_School"

Commission for Academic Accreditation

The **Commission for Academic Accreditation (CAA)** is the government-run institutional licensure and degree accreditation organization for private universities and their academic programmes in the United Arab Emirates (UAE). It was established in 1999, with headquarters in UAE's capital city Abu Dhabi, and is a department of the Ministry of Higher Education and Scientific Research. The CAA is a member of the Arab Network for Quality Assurance in Higher Education (ANQAHE)

The CAA has a number of commissioners led by its director, Dr Badr Aboul-Ela, a founder member of the organization. Institutions must follow standards set by the CAA. There are specific standards for e-learning and, since 2009, for vocational education and technical training. Licensure and accreditation are achieved through submission of supporting documentation and site visits by a commissioner and a visiting committee of experienced academics with appropriate expertise.

All non-federal higher education institutions operating outside a free-zone in the UAE must have a license to operate and their academic programmes must be accredited before students may be admitted. Many institutions operating within a free-zone nevertheless submit themselves to the CAA for license and accreditation.
Source (edited): "http://en.wikipedia.org/wiki/Commission_for_Academic_Accreditation"

Hamdan Bin Mohammed e-University

Hamdan Bin Mohammed e-University the first e-University in the United Arab Emirates, was officially inaugurated in February 2009. It is the successor of the e-TQM College which was initially inaugurated on September 30, 2002 by Sheikh Mohammed Bin Rashid Al Maktoum, Vice President, Prime Minister of the UAE and Ruler of Dubai.

Hamdan Bin Mohammed e-University comprises four main colleges, e-School of Business and Quality management, school of e-education, e-school of Health and Environmental studies and e-school of Continuing Education.

In addition to being accredited by national bodies and academic institutions, particularly the Ministry of Higher Education and Scientific Research in the UAE. Hamdan bin Mohammed e-University enjoys international associations with major educational institutions and universities, such as University of Bradford, University of Wisconsin, University of Huddersfield and the University of California, Berkeley.
Source (edited): "http://en.wikipedia.org/wiki/Hamdan_Bin_Mohammed_e-University"

Higher Colleges of Technology

The **Higher Colleges of Technology (HCT)** (in Arabic: كليات التقنية العليا) was established in 1988, and is the largest institution of higher learning in the United Arab Emirates (UAE) with over 19,000 students. During the 2009 - 2010 academic year there were 11,700 female and 6,500 male students enrolled at 17 campuses and 92 programs throughout the country. This number has increased for the current academic year. More than 48,000 UAE nationals are graduates of the institution.

The HCT provides post-secondary education in business, education, engineering technology, information technology, applied communications and health sciences.

The HCT places a strong emphasis on an innovative, project-driven and student-centred curriculum. English is used as the medium of instruction, with faculty recruited from around the world.

The HCT has formal alliances with a number of international tertiary education and training institutions, and corporate partnerships with local and multinational companies. Some programs have international accreditation: for example, the HCT's Bachelor of Education degree was developed with, and is certified by the University of Melbourne.

The CERT (Centre of Excellence for Applied Research and Training) is the commercial arm of the Higher Colleges of Technology, developing and providing education, training and applied technology for public and private sector clients. The Wharton Center for Family Business and Entrepreneurship Research for the Middle East is based at CERT. The University of Waterloo, Canada, offers dual degrees in collaboration with HCT through CERT.

The Chancellor of the HCT is His Excellency Sheikh Nahayan Mabarak Al Nahayan, also UAE Minister of Higher Education and Scientific Research. The Vice Chancellor, appointed in June 2005, is Dr Tayeb A. Kamali.

There are 17 campuses throughout the country, with separate colleges for male and female students. The central administration of the HCT is located in Abu Dhabi and includes the Vice Chancellor's Office, Office of the Provost (Dr Mark Drummond), Academic Central Services, Institutional Planning and Development (Dr. Senthil Nathan), Human Resource division (Dr. Rudolph Young), and Central Finance and IT services.

History

In 1985, HE Sheikh Nahayan Mabarak Al Nahayan, Chancellor of the United Arab Emirates University, made a commitment to establish a new system of postsecondary education for UAE Nationals that would stress the ideals of productivity, self-determination and excellence.

In fulfillment of that vision, the Higher Colleges of Technology (HCT) was established in 1988 by Federal Law No 2 issued by the Late Sheikh Zayed bin Sultan Al Nahyan, may his soul rest in peace.

In 1988 four colleges for men and women opened in Abu Dhabi and Al Ain, and in the next few years, men's and women's colleges were established in Dubai and Ras Al Khaimah. In 1997/1998 the Sharjah colleges for men and women were established in Sharjah's University City, followed by a women's college in Fujairah in 1999/2000 and a men's college in 2004/2005. Since 2006, new colleges have opened in Madinat Zayed and Ruwais. Additional facility expansion projects in 2006 included the new permanent facilities for Fujairah Men's College and Ras Al Khaimah Men's College.

Campuses

Abu Dhabi Men's College

Abu Dhabi Men's College (ADMC) opened in 1988 and has modern computer laboratories and technical workshops, and classrooms equipped with learning technology. ADMC offers a range of work-relevant programs in Business, Communication Technology, Engineering Technology, Health Sciences and Information Technology. The current director of the college is Dr Simon Jones.

ADMC is located adjacent to the HCT's Centre of Excellence for Applied Research and Training (CERT).

Abu Dhabi Women's College

Abu Dhabi Women's College (ADWC) opened in 1988. ADWC has 5 main teaching departments: Business, Applied Communication, Education, Health Sciences and Information Technology. ADWC also seeks to meet the needs of women who were unable to enter college directly after high school by offering a Work Readiness Program that prepares them for careers in private, public or self-owned companies. The wider community is serviced by Continuing Education programs which are open to the entire Abu Dhabi community. The present director of the college is Dr Christine Luscombe-Whyte.

Al Ain Men's College

Library at Al Ain Men's College

Al Ain Men's College (AAM) opened in 1988 with 61 students and 19 staff.

The college operated from a temporary campus in the Al Ain suburb of Sarooj until 1996 when a purpose built facility was opened on the road to the suburb of Zakher, near Al Ain Zoo. Athletics and other recreational facilities were completed in 2001. The campus has attractive gardens and dramatic views of Jebel Hafeet.

The college offers courses in business, engineering and information technology. In 2006 there were more than 700 students and 90 staff. The current director is Tim Smith, who is also director of Al Ain Women's College.

AAM recently announced the start of a new Executive MBA degree, the first for the city of Al Ain

Al Ain Women's College

Al Ain Women's College opened in 1988 and offers a wide variety of business and technical courses for Emirati women in Al Ain.

Dubai Men's College

Campus of Dubai Men's College

Dubai Men's College (DMC) opened in 1989 and offers programs in Business, Information Technology, Communication Technology and Engineering and awards Diploma, Higher Diploma and Bachelors degrees. More than 3000 students have graduated from the college and it currently enrolls approximately 2000 students and employs some 200 faculty and staff. In 2004 a new campus was established at Dubai Academic City and is equipped with state-of-the-art technologies and a wide range of sports, educational and recreational facilities.

DMC offers programs Communication Technology, Engineering, Business, Health Science and Information Technology including degree courses in Business Administration, Information Technology, Engineering Management, Construction Engineering and Communication Technology. Current director of the college is Dr Robert Richards.

Dubai Women's College

Dubai Women's College (DWC) opened in 1989 and offers courses in business, information technology, health science, communications technology and education and engineering DWC also hosts HCT's UNESCO Chair of Communication Technology and Journalism.

Enrolment at the DWC campus has increased from fewer than 200 to over 2,200 students in 2006. DWC relocated to a new, campus in the Al Quasis area of Dubai in 1998.

Dr Howard Reed has been Director of Dubai Women's College since 1992. In 2005, he was appointed to the Dubai Education Council, established by then Crown Prince, now Ruler of Dubai, Sheikh Mohammed bin Rashid Al Maktoum to improve the school education sector in Dubai.

Fujairah Men's College

Fujairah Men's College (FJM) opened in 2003 and offers a wide variety of business and technical courses for Emirati men in Fujairah. The Current director is Dr David Pelham who is also the director of Fujairah Women's College.

Fujairah Women's College

Fujairah Women's College (FJW) in 1999 and offers a wide variety of business and technical courses for Emirati women in Fujairah.

Ras Al Khaimah Men's College

Ras Al Khaimah Men's College (RKM) opened in 1993. The college was originally located in Ras Al Khaimah city on the site presently occupied by George Mason University. In 2004 it moved to Digdaga, before moving back to the city to its current campus in 2006. The campus is located in an area of Ras Al Khaimah known as Bererat. It is situated roughly 5 km from the city centre.

As a technical college, its courses focus on preparing its students for the workplace. It offers a Bachelor's Degree in e-Business Management, as well as Higher Diplomas and Diplomas in three subject areas: Mechatronics, Business and Information Technology.

The current director is Dr Robert Moulton who is also the Director of Ras Al Khaimah Women's College.

Ras Al Khaimah Women's College

Ras Al Khaimah Women's College (RKWC) has approximately 1200 students and offers a wide variety of business and technical courses for Emirati women in Ras Al Khaimah.

The Sharjah Higher Colleges of Technology

The Sharjah Higher Colleges of Technology (SHCT) are two of the sixteen colleges that comprise the Higher Colleges of Technology (HCT) in the United Arab Emirates (UAE). The **Sharjah Women's College** was established in 1997 and the **Sharjah Men's College** in 1998.

Located in University City in Sharjah, with separate campuses for males and females, the SHCT serve the post-secondary educational needs of the three neighboring emirates of Sharjah, Ajman, and Umm Al Quwain. Current enrolment at the Women's and Men's Colleges is 1,900 and 800 respectively (Sept. 2009). The SHCT employ over 300 staff from more than 25 different countries, with the great majority coming from English-speaking world.

The SHCT offer diploma, higher diploma, and bachelors level programs in Applied Communications, Business, Education, Engineering Technology, Health Sciences, and Information Technology. The language of instruction is English. The SHCT has a beautiful campus, with facilities that include well-equipped computer and other dedicated laboratories, an auditorium, a planetarium, and Olympic-size sports facilities.

The current and founding Director of the Sharjah Higher Colleges of Technology is Dr Farid Ohan (2009).

Madinat Zayed & Ruwais Colleges

New campus were opened in 2007 for both men and women in the western area of Abu Dhabi Emirate at Madinat Zayed and Ruwais. The Director of the MZ and Ruwais Colleges is Dr Phil Quirke.

HCT's Flagship Conferences

HCT's flagship conferences include:
- Education Without Borders (a biennial international student conference).
- Festival of Thinkers (a unique conference of interactions between young scholars and Nobel Laureates and World Thinkers).
- Global Entrepreneurship 2010 Conference (E2010).
- EWB Regional Forum for University Leaders (in North America, South Asia, Europe et al.).

Source (edited): "http://en.wikipedia.org/wiki/Higher_Colleges_of_Technology"

List of universities and colleges in the United Arab Emirates

This is a **list of universities in the United Arab Emirates**.
- [[Centre for Executive Education, Dubai Knowledge Village]]
- Abu Dhabi Men's College
- Abu Dhabi Women's College
- Abu Dhabi University
- Ajman University of Science and Technology
- Al Ain Men's College
- Al Ain Women's College
- Al Ghurair University
- American University in the Emirates
- American University of Asia
- American University in Dubai
- American University of Sharjah
- Birla Institute of Technology & Science, Pilani - Dubai
- Birla Institute of Technology International Centre, Ras Al Khaimah
- British University in Dubai - BUiD
- Canadian University Of Dubai
- Cass Business School
- CERT (Centre of Excellence for Applied Research and Training)
- Dubai Medical College for Girls
- Dubai Men's College
- Dubai Women's College
- Etisalat University College
- Fujairah College
- Fujairah Men's College
- Fujairah Women's College
- Gulf Medical College, now Gulf Medical University
- Hamdan Bin Mohammed e-University
- Heriot-Watt University Dubai
- Higher Colleges of Technology
- Ittihad University
- INSEAD Business School - Abudhabi
- Khalifa University of Science, Technology and Research
- London Business School
- NYU Abu Dhabi
- Ras Al Khaimah Men's College
- Ras Al Khaimah Women's College
- RAK Medical & Health Sciences University - College of Dental Sciences
- Rochester Institute of Technology

- Sharjah Men's College
- Sharjah Women's College
- Skyline College Sharjah
- Syracuse University
- United Arab Emirates University
- University of Sharjah
- University of Wollongong in Dubai
- Zayed University

Source (edited): "http://en.wikipedia.org/wiki/List_of_universities_and_colleges_in_the_United_Arab_Emirates"

Ministry of Higher Education and Scientific Research of the United Arab Emirates

The **Ministry of Higher Education and Scientific Research (MOHESR)** is a ministry of the government in the United Arab Emirates (UAE). Established in 1992, the Ministry has a number of departments, including the Commission for Academic Accreditation (CAA), which provides institutional licensure and degree accreditation for universities and their programmes in the UAE.

His Highness Sheikh Nahyan bin Mubarak Al Nahyan is the Minister of Higher Education and Scientific Research. He is also Chancellor of two of the UAE's three government-sponsored institutions of higher education, United Arab Emirates University and the Higher Colleges of Technology, and president of the third, Zayed University.

Source (edited): "http://en.wikipedia.org/wiki/Ministry_of_Higher_Education_and_Scientific_Research_of_the_United_Arab_Emirates"

National Research Foundation

The **National Research Foundation** is a foundation of the Ministry of Higher Education and Scientific Research in the United Arab Emirates. It has been designed to promote research activity in private and public universities and colleges, at centers of research in institutes and in companies, by individuals and by research teams in the United Arab Emirates.

History

In the United Arab Emirates (UAE), a National Research Foundation was created in March 2008, by a decree signed by Sheikh Nahyan bin Mubarak Al Nahyan, Minister of Higher Education & Scientific Research. The National Research Foundation is a Ministry of Higher Education & Scientific Research initiative intended to promote and coordinate research activity, to provide research leadership in the country and to provide funding support on a competitive basis to researchers based in the United Arab Emirates. In its early years, research projects that survive international peer review, that contribute social and economic benefits to the UAE and which enhance the development process in that country, have been favored.

Vision and mission

The vision of the NRF is stated as: "To support world-class research activities, and create an internationally competitive research environment and innovation system in the United Arab Emirates."

The mission of the NRF is: "To build an internationally competitive research capacity for the economic and social development of the United Arab Emirates"

It is intended that these research activities will enable the UAE to retain good scientists, to foster ideas and knowledge and to enable the businesses of the UAE to be more competitive and enhance the lives of its citizens.

NRF's objectives

Maintaining objectives are essential to advancing NRF's vision and the mission, they are:

- *Discovery:* develop and maintain a solid foundation of world-class research across a range of nationally relevant disciplines.
- *Linkage:* encourage and extend cooperative approaches to research between universities, government and industry.
- *Research Infrastructure:* increase the level and quality of research infrastructure in UAE.
- *Innovation and entrepreneurship:* contribute towards the building of an internationally competitive innovation system and culture of entrepreneurship in UAE.
- *Research education and training, and careers:* contribute to high-quality research education and training, and foster career opportunities for early career researchers, particularly UAE nationals.
- *Public engagement:* increase public and government awareness and understanding of the benefits of national research and the important results from NRF-funded projects.
- *Good governance:* implement best-practice governance and organizational structures consistent with transparency and accountability.

Source (edited): "http://en.wikipedia.org/wiki/National_Research_Foundation"